Padraic Colum

Twayne's English Authors Series

Kinley E. Roby, Editor
Northeastern University

TEAS 410

PADRAIC COLUM
(1881–1972)
Photograph courtesy of Padraic Colum Collection,
Glenn G. Bartle Library, State University
of New York at Binghamton

Padraic Colum

By Sanford Sternlicht

State University of New York at Oswego

Twayne Publishers • Boston

Padraic Colum

Sanford Sternlicht

Copyright © 1985 by G.K. Hall & Company
All Rights Reserved
Published by Twayne Publishers
A Division of G.K. Hall & Company
70 Lincoln Street
Boston, Massachusetts 02111

Kind permission has been granted
by the Macmillan Company
to quote from the works of Padraic Colum.

Book Production by Elizabeth Todesco
Book Design by Barbara Anderson

Printed on permanent/durable acid-free
paper and bound in the United States of
America.

Library of Congress Cataloging in Publication Data

Sternlicht, Sanford V.
    Padraic Colum.

    (Twayne's English authors series; TEAS 410)
    Bibliography: p. 157
    Includes index.
    1. Colum, Padraic, 1881–1972—Criticism and interpretation.
I. Title. II. Series.
PR6005.O38Z87   1985   821'.912   85-771
ISBN 0-8057-6901-3

Contents

About the Author
Preface
Chronology

Chapter One
The Patriot and the Exile   1

Chapter Two
Drama: The Promising Start   22

Chapter Three
The Poet in Ireland: 1902–1914   44

Chapter Four
The Irish-American Poet: 1914–1960   54

Chapter Five
The Images of Departure   85

Chapter Six
The Man of Letters:
Fiction, Biography, and Essays   106

Chapter Seven
A Gift for the Young:
Folklore, Mythology, and Books for Children   129

Chapter Eight
Achievement and Summation   144

Notes and References   151
Selected Bibliography   157
Index   162

About the Author

Sanford Sternlicht, Professor and Chairperson of the Department of Theatre at the State University of New York, College at Oswego, was formerly Professor of English and Director of Graduate Studies in English at that institution. A wide-range scholar-writer-director, Professor Sternlicht is the author of the following books: *Gull's Way* (poetry), 1961; *Love in Pompeii* (poetry), 1967; *The Black Devil of the Bayous* (history with E. M. Jameson), 1970; *John Webster's Imagery and the Webster Canon* (literary criticism), 1972; *McKinley's Bulldog: The Battleship Oregon* (history), 1977; *John Masefield* (Twayne English Authors Series), 1977; *C. S. Forester* (Twayne English Authors Series), 1981; and *U. S. F. Constellation: Yankee Racehorse* (history with E. M. Jameson), 1981. His many articles on subjects from Shakespeare to Graham Greene have appeared in *Renaissance Papers, Papers on Language and Literature, Minnesota Review, Harvard Magazine, Florida Review, College English, Ball State Forum, Midwest Quarterly, Calcutta Review, Studies in Humanities, Writers Digest,* etc. His poetry has appeared in over three hundred publications throughout the world, including the *New York Times,* the *New York Herald Tribune, Christian Science Monitor, Saturday Evening Post, Canadian Forum, Dalhousie Review,* and *Poetry Review* (London).

In 1960 Sanford Sternlicht received the *Writer Magazine* New Poets Award. The Poetry Society of America granted him a writing fellowship in 1965. The State University of New York Research Foundation awarded him fellowships and grants in 1963, 1964, 1965, 1969, and 1970.

Sanford Sternlicht was Leverhulme Visiting Fellow at the University of York, England, 1965–1966. He has also taught at Colgate University and occasionally teaches writing and drama in the English Department of Syracuse University.

Preface

As a young man in turn-of-the century Ireland, Padraic Colum was one of the leaders of the great Irish literary renaissance and one of the founders of the Irish National Theatre Society and the Abbey Theatre, along with William Butler Yeats, Lady Gregory, George Moore, AE (George Russell), and John Millington Synge. Disputes with Yeats and others, a growing interest and ability in lyric poetry, and the economic lure of America caused Colum to leave the Abbey and then Ireland. He left a theatre that would create a refulgence perhaps equal to the Comédie Française of Paris and the Moscow Art Theatre. If he had remained with the Abbey, he might have become a major dramatist of the twentieth century.

In America, ever the poet in exile, he was unable to adapt to the economics, aesthetics, and procedures of the commercial New York theatre. Instead of continuing as a dramatist, he perfected his lyric poetry and his gentle storytelling. He devoted a great part of his considerable gifts to writing folklore and children's books. This provided him with a comfortable living, if not with the opportunity to compete again in the world class genre of the drama. His ultimate contribution to literature would be as an Irish lyric poet.

In a way Colum had both the good fortune and bad luck to have been born in the right time and the right place. He was a talented young man at the moment when an emerging people were reaching for political freedom and literary greatness. He walked for a while with giants and they overshadowed him. But what company: Yeats, Joyce, and Synge!

Padraic Colum left them at the age of thirty-two, although he would make many trips to Dublin, London, and Paris to be with his friends and refresh his and their memories of Dublin before the Easter Rebellion of 1916 and the subsequent founding of the Irish Free State and the Irish Republic. He adopted United States citizenship, lived long and happily with "Molly," his critic-journalist wife, and became known as *the* Irish-American poet, the gentle, aging writer who lived through and was untouched by all the radical poetry movements of the twentieth century.

A knowledge and appreciation of the life and work of Padraic Colum afford three rewards: first, to understand the drive that motivated a young, rural Irishman at the turn of the century to write for and participate in the struggle for freedom and identity is to understand the impetus behind the Irish literary renaissance and the Irish Revolution; second, a study of Colum presents a psychological guide to the effects of exile, even self-imposed exile, on a nationalistic writer emotionally attached to the land, significant because exile has been the lot and the fate of so many twentieth-century writers; third, appreciating the lyric beauty of Colum's verse reminds the reader of the validity and endurance of conservative, mainstream English poetry.

One thing more: Colum was a true and good friend of many fellow artists, particularly James Joyce, who said of him: "he has the strange thing called genius." That genius alternately ebbed and flooded, eventually leaving for posterity a few fine peasant plays, an excellent body of lyric and dramatic poetry, and insightful memoirs of life in a special place and time: the Dublin of James Joyce's Stephen Dedalus and Leopold Bloom. Thus, because he knew everybody and forgot nothing, because he was there when a great literature was reborn and an ancient people were about to win their freedom, and because he contributed to both events, his place in literary history is assured.

Padraic Colum thought of himself as a man of letters, one who could produce works of art in any genre. Furthermore, literature was a way through which he could maintain his Irish roots, the source of his creative powers. Despite his frequent trips to Ireland from America and despite carefully maintained friendships with key Irish figures in the arts and government, time and distance ultimately weakened those roots and diminished those powers.

Nevertheless, he succeeded in becoming a significant part of the new literature of a reborn people through his contributions to the emerging Irish National Theatre: *Broken Soil* (1903), *The Land* (1905), and *Thomas Muskerry* (1910); through his epic Irish novels: *Castle Conquer* (1923) and *The Flying Swans* (1957); and, most of all, through his poetry, which celebrates a time and a place and people, singing with clarity, precision, simplicity, and great beauty.

I am particularly indebted to Zack Bowen for his seminal study; *Padraic Colum* (1970), and for his patient interviewing of the poet in the 1960s, the tapes of which, along with other materials, were made available to me by the Special Collections staff of the Glen G. Bartle

Preface

Library of the State University of New York at Binghamton. Also I thank the interlibrary loan staffs of Byrd Library of Syracuse University and Penfield Library of State University of New York at Oswego. Finally, I am grateful to Mrs. Joanne Jones and other colleagues in the Department of Theatre at the College of Oswego.

Sanford Sternlicht

State University of New York at Oswego

Chronology

1881 Born Patrick Collumb on 8 December at Collumbkille, County Longford, Ireland; firstborn of eight children of Patrick Collumb, master of a workhouse, and Susan MacCormack Collumb, daughter of a gardener.

1891 Family moves to Sandy Cove, near Dublin, where Colum's father obtained work as a railway clerk. Colum begins eight years of formal education at the Glasthule National (public) School in Sandy Cove.

1897 Mother dies and family begins to break up.

1901 Joins the Gaelic League and the Irish Republican Army. Begins to call himself Padraic Colum. Meets James Joyce.

1902 First poems published in the *Irish Independent* and *United Irishman.* Joins the Irish National Dramatic Company and meets William Butler Yeats.

1903 Irish National Theatre Society produces *Broken Soil* at Molesworth Hall.

1904 Gives up job to devote his life to writing.

1905 Irish National Theatre Society produces *The Land* at the Abbey Theatre.

1907 Theatre of Ireland Company produces *The Fiddler's House,* a rewrite of *Broken Soil,* in the Rotunda. *Wild Earth* and *Other Poems.*

1908 Receives five-year scholarship from Thomas Hughes Kelly to pursue writing. Theatre of Ireland Company produces *The Miracle of the Corn* at the Abbey Theatre.

1910 Irish National Theatre Society produces *Thomas Muskerry* at the Abbey Theatre.

1911 Co-founder of the *Irish Review.*

1912 Marries Mary Gunning Maguire.

1914 The Colums emigrate to the United States.

1916 *The King of Ireland's Son.* American edition of *The Wild Earth.*

1922 *Dramatic Legends,* and *Other Poems.* Returns to Ireland for first of frequent, long visits.

1923 *Castle Conquer.*

1924 *At the Gateways of the Day.*

1925 *The Bright Islands.* First permanent home in New Canaan, Connecticut

1927 *Creatures.*

1929 *Balloon.*

1930 *Old Pastures.* Moves to France.

1932 *Poems.*

1933 Returns to America to take up permanent residence in Manhattan.

1937 *Legends of Hawaii.*

1939 *Flower Pieces.* Begins teaching at Columbia University.

1943 *The Frenzied Prince.*

1953 *Collected Poems.*

1957 Mary Colum dies. *The Flying Swans.*

1958 *Irish Elegies. Our Friend James Joyce* (written with Mary).

1959 *Ourselves Alone: Arthur Griffith and the Origins of the Irish Free State.*

1960 *The Poet's Circuits.*

1966 Lantern Theatre in Dublin produces *The Challengers.*

1967 *Carricknabauna* produced off-Broadway.

1969 *Images of Departure.*

1972 Padraic Colum dies in Enfield, Connecticut, on 11 January; age 90. His body is flown to Dublin for burial.

Chapter One
The Patriot and the Exile

Padraic Colum, a writer with several audiences, led three distinct lives: the genial Irish bard; the hard-working author of a stream of children's books, travel essays, and folklore studies; and the historical participant, along with his wife, the critic Mary Colum, in the belletristic world of English-language literature through more than half of the twentieth century. It was a world with four capitals: New York, London, Dublin, and Paris. But for Colum everything emanated from this matrix: he was an Irish Catholic who descended from peasant farmers. They were men and women who loved a land. So did Colum—for a lifetime.

Birth

On 8 December 1881, in Longford in the Irish Midlands, a son, the first of eight children, was born to Patrick Collumb, a graduate of the national school and a teacher in the Longford workhouse, and his wife, Susan MacCormack Collumb. The child, born in the workhouse where his parents resided, was given his father's name: Patrick Collumb.[1]

The Ireland into which young Patrick was born was still very much a feudal country. Except for the Pale around Dublin, then and now very much an eighteenth-century city, it was a country of great manor houses owned by wealthy Anglo-Irish Protestants, who thought themselves as much British as Irish and who spent much of their time in London; and a country of innumerable tenant farmhouses and small holdings peopled by a poor, deeply religious Catholic people who longed for political and cultural independence from England. Ireland was a conquered country, albeit one conquered long ago by a people not among the cruelest of the world. The Irish had much personal freedom, and if a slave mentality endured, it was because of difficult economic conditions: high rents for absentee-owned farms and little cash for crops and cottage industry. The wealthy few generally disdained the country people who were peasants in all but name, and the country people were often self-loathing.[2]

Patrick's father, a heavy-drinker, found his salary as a teacher, and then master of the workhouse, inadequate to support a wife and eight children. Deeply in debt, he resigned his position, left his family to live with Susan's mother's family in County Cavan, and traveled to the American West in search of fortune. All he could manage was a cattle-handling job shipping animals from Colorado to New York, and then work shoveling snow in the bitter winter of New York City, until he limped home to take a position as a clerk in the Sandy Cove Railway Station near Dublin.[3] His story was not unusual. Indeed, some families were proud to boast that no one in their number had had to leave Ireland. It meant they were managing to cope and keep together.

Many families were also deeply divided over how to relate to the English; some advocated joining the government and assimilating, citing the foolishness of attempting to resist the world's mightiest empire, while others fiercely argued for resistance to English rule and culture. It was not unusual for one son to serve in the British army while another would be working for Irish independence. Indeed, Patrick's brother, Fred, served first in the British army and then became a petty officer in the Royal Navy. He was injured in World War I and died shortly afterwards.

Childhood

The Collumb family had originally come from Collumbkille, an ancient seat. Patrick's father was the first to break from the land. While he was in America, however, his eldest son came under the influence of the boy's uncle, Micky Burns, Susan's brother-in-law, a man who earned his living by purchasing fowl from farmers and re-selling them in towns. Young Patrick sometimes was allowed to travel the countryside with his uncle. On these trips he came to know the roads of Ireland about which he would later write. Also his uncle had a fine voice and a large repertoire of songs and yarns to beguile an impressionable lad not yet nine years old. Previously, before moving to County Cavan, the boy had listened with rapt attention to the tales of ancient Ireland told by the poor, old, disabled, and sometimes ill peasants who lived for a time in the workhouse of Longford.[4]

Then father returned from America and regrouped his family, Susan and the children: Patrick, Frederick, Eilleen, Donald, Maisy (who died an infant), Richard, another Maisy, and a Susan; and young Patrick began school at the Glasthule National School in Sandy Cove. His father, having become stationmaster, obtained work for Patrick as a railway delivery boy.[5]

School was a great delight for Patrick. A fine schoolmaster, Denis Condon, introduced the promising lad to a serious study of poetry, and the boy used most of his meager spending money on secondhand books. His formal education lasted only eight years, until he was seventeen. Then he passed a railway examination and was appointed to a clerkship in the Irish Railway Clearing House on Kildare Street in Dublin. His work day was nine hours long, six days a week. After work he would settle down to write poetry and then plays.[6]

Meanwhile, Patrick's mother had died in 1897 and the family dispersed to various relations in the country. His father lost his job due to overimbibing and Patrick undertook to help his younger brother and sisters financially. He would journey to the north and west to visit his siblings whenever he could.

Dublin

Young Patrick, the lad from the country, was amazed and overwhelmed by the seemingly frenzied activity of the city. Although Dublin was not a huge metropolis like London, still it offered varied cultural and intellectual opportunities. Movements bristled everywhere:

dramatic, artistic, educational; there were movements for the restoration of the Irish language, for reviving native arts and crafts, for preserving ancient ruins, for resurrecting native costume, an array of political movements; here, too, were the theaters and the tearooms and pubs which corresponded to the café life of the Continental city.[7]

The great excitements for an aspiring writer were literary. The writings of the time were not oneiric floatings but rousing expressions of nationalistic fervor. Patrick haunted the National Library. He observed the many university students and was anxious to make their acquaintance and learn from them:

James Joyce was very noticeable among the crowd of students who frequented the National Library or who sauntered along the streets between Nelson's Pillar and Stephen's Green. He was tall and slender when I knew him first, with a Dantesque face and steely blue eyes. The costume I saw him in as I look back includes a peaked cap and tennis shoes more or less white.[8]

At the age of twenty Patrick Columb joined the Gaelic League, thus committing himself to the development of Irish culture as well as the promotion of the Irish language; and he joined the Irish Republican Brotherhood, thus committing himself to Irish independence. Later he began secret, illegal, Irish Republican Army military drills with his friend Arthur Griffith, the journalist and revolutionary leader who had founded the important paper, the *United Irishman,* and would help to establish the Sinn Fein political party. Long after Griffith's death, his younger friend would write his biography.

Now Patrick began to use the name Padraic Colum; Padraic, the Gaelic form of Patrick, first like the poet–revolutionary, Padraic Pearse, who would die a martyr in the Easter Uprising of 1916; and Colum, a phonetic spelling of his surname as well as, of course, a reference to the dove and to the ancient Irish poet-saint, St. Colum (as pronounced in Gaelic). However, Padraic remained Patrick to his intimates[9] and he never did learn much Gaelic despite attending the enthusiastic meetings of the league.[10] Still, to be an Irish poet with two saints in your name!

First Publication

In 1902 Colum's poetry began to be published in the *Irish Independent* and Griffith's *United Irishman.* Many of the earliest poems were fiery nationalistic pieces, which, Colum later said, were well lost. Other pieces, those that portrayed the country people Colum knew so well, are among his best short works. William Butler Yeats, Ireland's greatest poet, read and admired the poems and some one-act plays in the *United Irishman,* and went to meet Colum at the Irish National Clearing House and praise him. Recognition by Yeats established the young railway clerk as a part of the Dublin literary scene. At this time also, the poet AE (George Russell) discovered Colum and made him a disciple. AE, not Yeats, would be the great poetic influence on Colum.

Colum was writing short plays for publication rather than performance because for all practical purposes there was no indigenous Irish theater, Dublin having but three professional theaters all hosting English companies playing English dramas. His early, short plays were written for the *Irish Independent* and *United Irishman* in 1902.[11] One of them, *The Saxon Shillin'*, won a three guineas prize offered by an Irish literary society called *Cumann na nGaedeal* of which Colum was a member. The prize was for a play that would help discourage young Irishmen from joining the British army. The Boer War, Britain's South African Viet Nam, was winding down but still left a bad taste in the mouths of many Irishmen who had supported the Boer farmers in their losing struggle for independence against the British Empire. Irishmen were, in fact, fighting on both sides.

The Saxon Shillin' took as its title a derisive expression used by some Irishmen to imply selling out to the English by joining the British forces. To "take the King's shilling" meant that one had agreed to enlist. Colum, himself was close to this problem as his brother Fred had joined up. Because of this provocative play, Frank Fay, who had called for an Irish national theater in the pages of *United Irishman,* and his brother Willie (W.G.) Fay (both aspiring actors) invited Colum to join their newly formed Irish National Dramatic Company as an actor as well as a playwright.

The Saxon Shillin' was scheduled to be performed in 1902, but was withdrawn by Willie Fay. Colum later said: "Willie Fay declined it on the ground that the main situation could not be staged effectively. But there were those in the Society who thought that his refusal to have anything to do with the production came from the fact that he did not want to have the garrison deployed against the hopeful theatre enterprise."[12] However, the one-act play was finally performed on 15 May 1903 by others after Colum reluctantly agreed to revise and soften the ending. The change, however, angered his friend Griffith and also the great Irish woman revolutionary, Maud Gonne.

Meanwhile, Yeats, Lady Isabella Augusta Gregory, George Moore, and Edward Martyn had founded the Irish Literary Theatre in 1899, the true beginning of modern Irish drama if not of modern Irish theater, an honor which belongs to the Abbey Theatre.[13] At the Ancient Concert Rooms they produced Yeats's *Countess Kathleen* and Martyn's *Heather Field.* Other productions followed at the Gaiety Theatre, but the company was unsure of itself and fractious; it had got off to a rocky start. The Fays' group appeared on the scene and seemed to have more vitality, better actors, and a greater chance of success.

Yeats consulted with Lady Gregory and then offered the Fays his
Kathleen Ni Houlihan to be performed on the same bill with AE's
(George Russell) *Deirdre.* The Fays accepted and all joined forces.

The Irish National Theatre Society

Yeats persuaded his friend, Maud Gonne, to play the title role in
Kathleen ni Houlihan, and the Fays managed to obtain free use of St.
Teresa's Temperance Hall in Clarendon Street for the nights of 2, 3,
4 April 1902.[14] Recognizing the historical and artistic significance of
the occasion, English critics were in attendance. The audience was
stunned by the beauty and acting strength of Maud Gonne. The run
was a great success. Padraic Colum performed the role of Buinne, son
of Fergus in *Deirdre.*

A new drama society was formed immediately to capitalize on the
success. It was to be called The Irish National Dramatic Company
and then The Irish National Theatre Society. AE was elected first
president. He declined in favor of Yeats, who accepted.[15] A truly vi-
able national theater had been created. It would shortly lead to the
formation of the great Abbey Theatre Company.

Major Plays

In 1903, at Molesworth Hall, Colum played in Yeats's *The Hour
Glass* and *The King's Threshold,* but with the critically successful production of his play, *Broken Soil,* on 3 December 1903, Colum was
relegated exclusively to the role of writer.

One Dubliner who did not like Colum's play was James Joyce with
whom he had established a friendship that would last until Joyce's
death in 1941. Colum remembered with amusement:

Joyce asked me to let him see the script. I did. Afterward he said, "I do not
know from which of them you derive the most misunderstanding—Ibsen or
Maeterlinck. . . . Rotten from the foundation up."[16]

The company, however, needed a suitable, permanent home.[17] Molesworth Hall was no longer acceptable. They tried a short tour to London to gain recognition and, perhaps, financial support. There the
Irish plays were well received, especially *Broken Soil.* A wealthy En-

glish friend of Yeats, Miss Elizabeth Horniman, now came forth with a generous offer to purchase a theater for the company. The tiny Mechanics Theatre on Abbey Street was obtained, along with the disused morgue next door, and on 27 December 1904, the long, great Abbey tradition began. Colum was one of the twenty signers of the agreement between the company and Miss Horniman for the Abbey Theatre. Although the play that opened the Abbey was, naturally, one of Yeats's, *On Baile's Strand*, it was Colum's *The Land*, first performed on 9 June 1905, that gave the theater its initial success. One reason that Yeats and Colum had a falling out shortly afterwards may have been that the great poet was jealous because the Dublin audiences consistently preferred Colum's peasant plays to his symbolic, poetic dramas. Colum, however, remained a great admirer of Yeats for his entire life.

Joseph Holloway, that irrepressible Dublin playgoer, was in the house at the opening of *The Land:*

Friday, June 9. A goodly crowd of patrons put in an appearance at the Abbey Theatre where Padraic Colum's three act play, *The Land*, was produced for the first time on any stage . . . I must say at once that the new piece was received with genuine enthusiasm. The actors were recalled after each act, and the author at the end of the play. He came forward and shyly bowed, returning hurriedly as if scared by the sight of the audience. Colum is a strange lad and always looks to me as if a good square meal would do him a world of good. A slight, fragile scrap of humanity with the look of a startled fawn ever hovering about his eyes.[18]

Thus Padraic Colum was a major figure in the development and the success of the Abbey Theatre, an institution which made one of the great contributions to dramatic literature in the twentieth century. Its importance can only be matched by the Moscow Art Theatre which was established in 1898 and, perhaps, the Théâtre Libre of Paris, which was established in 1887. The outstanding playwrights of the Abbey, besides Colum, were Yeats, Lady Gregory, John Millington Synge, and, later, Sean O'Casey.

The original theater sat 536 people. The proscenium opening was 21 feet wide. The wall-to-wall width was 40 feet. The stage depth from curtain line to the back wall was only 16 feet, 4 inches.[19] So the writers of the company were constrained to write small-cast plays with limited scenic requirements. Scenes had to be fairly intimate and, of great importance, the emphasis had to be on the word.

The Abbey Company, under Yeats's leadership, struck out against English rule, religious hypocrisy, Irish complacency, and sentimental nationalism. Its most controversial production was Synge's *The Playboy of The Western World* on 26 January 1907, before a full house, many of whom came to jeer the efforts of the provocative playwright. The audience, at first pleased, was soon outraged at the less-than-ideal depiction of the Irish character. The mention of the word *shift*, a woman's undergarment, was the match that lighted the fuse and a riot exploded. People fought all over the house. The next day the public demanded that the show be closed, but Yeats and the company refused. The police were called in by Yeats for the remainder of the week's run and thus more fighting was provoked. Colum and others thought that it was a mistake to bring in police. Colum's father, fortified like many with a few snorts, was one of the battlers. He was arrested, carted off, and convicted as one of the nationalists disturbing the peace.[20]

The controversy followed the company on tour to London and America, but Yeats and Synge prevailed. Synge, with his unerring ability to portray rural Irish character, and O'Casey, the later genius of Irish urban character, would prove to be the most enduring of the Abbey's playwrights; it is their plays that continue on the worldwide living stage. Alas, Synge, ill and besieged, died only two years after the opening of *The Playboy of The Western World*. He was only thirty-eight years old.

And there was another controversy beside the battle between the company and a section of the public; it was the internal conflict. From the beginning Yeats wanted the national drama of Ireland to be "high toned." It was to be a deeply symbolic verse drama.[21] It was to stand as a peak of renewed Irish creativity. He naturally saw the new theater as an extension of what was to be called the "Celtic Revival." He also wanted to "shape" the audience by charging a somewhat high minimum admission that would make it difficult for students and the poorer people to attend, thus packing the house with an audience potentially more receptive to Symbolist drama. On the other side, Colum and Synge and most of the audience wanted realistic prose plays about contemporary Irish life, themes, and problems. Colum resigned. Synge died. But there was no final victory for either side, to the betterment of Irish drama.

Break with the Abbey
and Publication of *Wild Earth*

Fed up with what he saw as dictatorial actions by Yeats, the Fays, and Miss Horniman, the proud Colum left the Irish National Theatre Company and joined a maverick organization called The Theatre of Ireland, which produced *The Fiddler's House* in 1907 in the Rotunda, and Colum's weak verse play, *The Miracle of The Corn,* in 1908. Lady Gregory tried to get Colum to return to the Society, using kind words and predicting that he would regret a permanent estrangement. She was right. The same year, 1907, Colum's first book of verse, *Wild Earth,* was published in Dublin and was well received. He was developing a double reputation: playwright and poet.

Holloway's journal seems to have recorded Colum's artistic ambivalence at the time:

Monday, December 10. Mr. Padraic Colum enticed a great number to the National Literary Society rooms by the bait of a lecture on "National Drama" only to disappoint them by speaking on "Lyric Poetry."[22]

An American philanthropist, Thomas Hughes Kelly, gave the young writer a scholarship to pursue his craft. The money enabled Colum to concentrate on poetry, but he did write one more play in Ireland, *Thomas Muskerry,* which the Abbey accepted and then produced on 5 May 1910.

Courtship and Marriage

In 1909 Padraic Colum met Mary Gunning Maguire, his beloved "Molly." With a vast cloud of red-gold hair, she was a strikingly beautiful, recent graduate of University College, Dublin, trying to make her way in the heady world of Irish arts and letters, which was then, as it is now, a man's world. Molly was a suffragist; at the same time she taught at Padraic Pearse's school, St. Enda's. They courted for three years and were married in midsummer 1912.[23] They were deeply and romantically in love. A surviving letter from Padraic to Molly surely expresses the true tone of the relationship.

2 Frankfort Place

Dear Old Moll
I waited until 3 O'c . . .
I must see you tomorrow. I'll call about 2:30.
I think that would be the right time to make a call. I'll don my new suit
and look very respectable, and I'll bring my "Wild Earth" to Mrs. Earl.
Dear old girl I send my love to you until we meet to-morrow. Do you think
you could come out with me . . . I was thinking of you all day. Isn't it
grand we're in love with each other. Nothing can come between us.

> Good bye darling girl
> Patrick[24]

The marriage was an ideal one. Molly was a fine critic, a perceptive
observer of human nature, and a lover of good company. She was fas-
cinated by famous people in all walks of life. They, in turn, were
bemused by the tiny, attractive woman, whose lovely face belied an
incisive wit. As critic (*From These Roots*, 1937), biographer, and journalist she earned widespread respect.

As Colum was generally, humble, reticent, and whimsical, her
confident high-seriousness proved an efficacious complement to his
personality. Together they were first a young, witty, verbal, good-
looking couple. Later, they were an urbane, well-traveled pair of
professional writers with friends all over the world welcoming them
for their wisdom, experience, and good company. In old age they
were a white-haired, heavy, and formidable pair, more concerned
with soul than with body, together forty-eight years until Molly's
death in 1957 at the age of seventy-three.

After the marriage they honeymooned in England and then returned to Dublin, almost without funds, to try to earn a livelihood
in the Irish literary world. In the year before their marriage Colum
had helped to found an important, new literary periodical, the *Irish
Review*. Other founders included Thomas MacDonagh and David
Houston of Padraic Pearse's teaching staff. Molly, also one of the
teachers, managed to obtain some assignments too. Among the early
contributors were George Moore, AE, and Pearse. Colum held the
editorship from 1912 through 1913. The *Irish Review* ran until November 1914, dying just after Colum left Ireland.[25] MacDonagh and

Pearse, revolutionaries both, would soon find martyrdom before English firing squads in the immediate aftermath of Easter, 1916.

The living for the Colums wasn't easy. Padriac had long ago committed himself to literature. He would earn their way by words or break in the trying. The *Freeman's Journal* and the *Irish Times* paid him for editorials; the English publications *Manchester Guardian* and *New Statesman* bought articles. The theater brought in very little money, especially since the Theatre of Ireland Company was not successfully competing with the Irish National Dramatic Company. Colum only received one pound a week when a play of his was on the boards.[26] Holloway reports seeing Colum selling some of his personal library to a book dealer and bargaining very hard.[27]

Hard work, struggle, concern for determining Irish politics, and maturity were tempering Colum and molding him to look like what he was always to be: The Poet. In 1913, eight years after his initial description of the hungry young playwright, Holloway described the professional poet in his own home at 2 Belville Ave, Donnybrook:

What a strange and wonderful head is Colum's with its big, half dome-like forehead and large, velvety soft sad eyes under curved brows with long straggling locks of hair falling anyhow over forehead and ears. . . . A strikingly delicate face, with thin hollow cheeks and drawn sad expression. A poet to the eye![28]

At this time Colum was very upset over the growing possibility of civil war in Ireland. Unionists in the north were arming, and those like Colum, who supported Home Rule, were angry and frightened. The Irish Volunteers was formed to counter the Ulster Volunteers and thus two underground armies were created. Colum joined the Irish Volunteers and participated in illegal gunrunning. A rifle became a frequent companion.

The Kelly funds had come to an end. Although the Colums enjoyed the artistic milieu of Dublin and their camaraderie with many of the finest writers in the Anglo-Irish world of literature, they simply could not survive on the income from belletristic activities and free-lance journalism. Lady Gregory, one of The Abbey's managers, quashed plans to produce a new play by Colum, *The Betrayal,* in order to substitute one of her own.[29] In Ireland the future looked bleak for the newlyweds.

Emigration to America

Meanwhile, Colum's aunt in Pittsburgh, Josephine Colum, had offered a honeymoon trip to America which had been declined. The offer was renewed and accepted. The penurious couple set out for the New World via Liverpool, but the "Guns of August" had been fired and the trip on a British liner in wartime was harrowing. The Colums only intended a visit, expecting to return to Dublin for New Year's. They never dreamed that they were going to a new life in a new country of which one day they would become citizens.

In Pittsburgh they stayed with Colum's aunt and Padraic made a little money lecturing and reading poetry. To his delight, he realized that Americans knew about and were very interested in the Irish Revival. This fact would be a mainstay of his life; he would always be the poet from Dublin, who had known "everyone." The Carnegie School of Drama was producing contemporary Irish plays including Colum's and he was paid to advise the productions.

After three months in Pittsburgh, the Colums began to plan their return to Ireland, but were persuaded to spend some time in New York City before leaving. Also Irish friends urged them not to return until the war was over. In the autumn of 1914 most people believed World War I would last only a few months.

The Colums moved to New York and rented a dingy room on Beekman Place, not then a fashionable address. Colum soon realized that he could be a great help to the cause of Irish independence by lecturing and writing for the Irish community in America. British officials did what they could to interfere with Colum's work. Writing for the *Gaelic American,* however, reached and touched the entire Irish community in North America.

Padraic and Molly, always very sociable, managed pretty much to duplicate their Dublin lifestyle in Manhattan. They quickly made many good friends in the literary and publishing world. They were a handsome, witty couple, always good company and loyal. Colum joined the Poetry Society of America, where he would later meet and hit it off with Robert Frost. The two would remain close friends for much of their lifetimes.

A lecture tour in the Middle West brought an opportunity for a long visit in Chicago at the home of Harriet Moody, the wealthy widow of the poet William Vaughn Moody.[30] The Midwest school of American poetry now opened up to Colum and welcomed the Irish writer. New friends included Carl Sandburg, Edgar Lee Masters, Sherwood Anderson, Vachel Lindsay, and Harriet Monroe, the founder of *Poetry*, the little Chicago magazine that would become the most influential poetry publication in the United States. Later, in the East and in France they would come to know and establish long-term friendships with Edwin Arlington Robinson, Van Wyck Brooks, Amy Lowell, Somerset Maugham, and Elinor Wylie.

In the fall of 1915 the Colums returned to New York. The raging European war precluded going back to Dublin. They were poor and on their own again, struggling in a boardinghouse existence, publishing short pieces in periodicals, tutoring, and occasionally lecturing. Mary got work with the garment industry periodical, *Women's Wear*. Unfortunately, Padraic, even with his wife's help, was unable to earn a living by his serious writing. Finally, something happened in Padraic Colum's life that would change the direction of his work, provide a lifelong living, and particularly divert him from his expressed calling: creator of significant literature. Most unfortunately, it would change the perception of him that contemporary critics would hold, from serious man of letters to children's writer. Colum received a very modest offer of eight dollars per week for a regular contribution of short stories for the children's column of the New York *Sunday Tribune*. He was glad to have even this small, regular income, and, as a childless man with many nieces and nephews, surely he was also pleased with the role of uncle-storyteller.

Children's Literature

A Hungarian illustrator, Willy Pogány, informed Colum that he was interested in illustrating a book of Irish stories for children.[31] Using the pieces in the *Tribune* as a base, they collaborated on *The King of Ireland's Son* (1916). It was published by Holt, Pogány's regular publisher, and that company also agreed to bring out an American edition of *Wild Earth*. Thus, in one year, Colum had two successful books in print in America. *The King of Ireland's Son* established his ability to write effective prose for children, and *Wild Earth* brought him critical recognition in American poetry circles.

Meanwhile, the editors of Macmillan were impressed by *The King of Ireland's Son* (which later they would buy from Holt and reissue), and they felt that Colum should be in their "stable." In return for an annual salary he would produce two books per year for them: one a children's treatment of one of the world's great sagas or myths; the other, a collection of stories for younger children. At last, Colum, at age thirty-four, had attained that elusive goal: a steady income. Also the McDowell Colony in Peterboro, New Hampshire, provided free summer residence for the Colums in 1917 and 1918, and again in 1923. During these summers Colum worked hard on his first novel, *Castle Conquer* (1923). The thought of a permanent return to Ireland ebbed away in the wash of success and the exciting New York literary life, although the Colums anguished over Ireland's trauma in 1916 and the death of Padraic Pearse and Roger Casement and many other revolutionaries they had known and worked with.

Ireland was undergoing an ordeal by fire. Padraic Colum, the Irish Volunteer and gunrunner of 1913, did what he could in America for the cause of Irish independence. The British execution of the surviving leaders of the 1916 uprising, except for the American-born Eamon de Valera, achieved the main goal of the insurgents: it galvanized the Irish people into resistance and then open warfare. The Anglo-Irish war ensued, resulting in agreement, in 1921, on the creation of the Irish Free State and the partition of Ireland. But the Irish Civil War followed over the terms of the peace treaty, and brother killed brother in the bloodbath. Colum's old friend, Arthur Griffith, one of the treaty negotiators, collapsed and died from exertion, tension, anxiety, and disappointment. The new Irish National Army crushed the now-outlawed Irish Republican Army in pitched battles.

First Visit to Ireland

Ireland had to pass through a maelstrom, and well-meaning expatriates like Colum could only look on helplessly. When the war ground down and fighting sputtered away in 1922, Colum realized, as Molly and he sailed home for their first visit in eight years, that the Ireland of his youth was gone, yet safe in his own mind and heart. He would spend his life writing about the old Ireland. He would be its bard and chronicler, but he would do so from the New World. The time of "the troubles" belonged to other writers.

Back in Ireland, Colum was treated as something of a hero. The government of the newly independent nation was well aware of how important American public opinion was in their freedom struggle, and they were no less aware of Colum's part in shaping that pro-Irish opinion and marshaling the Irish-American community. After all, de Valera had raised five million dollars for the cause on one American trip alone. The Colums were welcomed by the new president of the Free State, William Cosgrave, and the commander of the victorious National Army, General Richard Mulcahy. Although Colum grieved for Griffith, who briefly had served as president, and who would have greeted Colum had he survived,[32] assuaging the grief was the delightful fact that there wasn't a Union Jack in sight. Instead, the Irish Tricolor flew everywhere.

The visit was only for a few months, but Colum managed to get a play on at the Abbey, *The Grasshopper,* written with E. Washburn Freund, and produced on 24 October 1922. While Molly visited in London, Colum went out to rural Ireland again and traveled the by-ways to renew his memory of the land he loved. His best anecdotal book on the Irish countryside, *The Road Round Ireland* (1926), partly resulted from this trip.

Colum joined his wife in London, and then they both went over to Paris to visit James Joyce, but the novelist was himself traveling. However, Ezra Pound was there to greet them. Pound and Joyce had become friends after Colum had arranged an introduction for his Irish friend. The erratically brilliant American poet was another lifelong friend, although Colum was already quite aware of Pound's disturbing qualities.[33] Many years later, in Canto LXXX, Pound would lament Colum's perceived, declining creative power:

> Whoi didn't he (Padraic Colum)
> Keep on writing at that voltage. . . .

International Writer

The Colums returned to New York, only to entrain, almost immediately, for San Francisco, there to board a ship for Honolulu. Colum had received an exciting assignment:

The Hawaiian Legislature had formed a Commission on Myth and Folklore; the function of the Commission was to have a survey made of the stories for children—primarily for the children of the Hawaiian Islands. By an arrangement made between the Commission and the Yale University Press, I was invited to make the survey and to reshape the stories.[34]

Colum found it necessary to visit the most remote parts of several islands. He worked very hard both in the Bishop Museum and in the field. In three months, to his own surprise, he was lecturing to Hawaiians on their own traditions, although he modestly claimed to know "nothing" about the business.[35]

Three folklore books resulted from this brief trip: *At the Gateways of the Day* (1924), *The Bright Islands* (1925), and finally *Legends of Hawaii* (1937), a one-volume combination of the first two books. Colum now had an established reputation as a folklorist. Also in the Hawaiian year Macmillan brought out *Dramatic Legends and Other Poems* (1922) and, the next year, his first novel, *Castle Conquer* (1923).

After Hawaii, the Colums made another trip to Ireland, France, and Italy. In Dublin Colum met Sean O'Casey and saw the Abbey Theatre perform O'Casey's *Shadow of a Gunman*. "Colum was present in the front row of the stalls . . . and he became so excited during the events, in the second act, that he kept unconsciously jumping up and down in his seat, and even at times went over to the stage front and placed his elbows on the stage ledge as he gazed intently at what was taking place thereon."[36]

He must surely have realized that in O'Casey the Irish National Drama had produced a world-class playwright, at least the equal of his old companion Synge. Characteristically, Colum was not jealous. His rapt attention and almost childlike delight indicated his deep appreciation for the skill and artistry of O'Casey.

In Paris Colum was very happy to see his friend "Jice" again. He had last seen James Joyce in Dublin in 1912, just before the angry novelist went into voluntary exile.[37] Colum had tried to help his friend achieve Irish publication of *Dubliners* but had failed. In America Colum, among the very first—perhaps just after Joyce himself—to recognize the novelist's great genius, had tried to help Joyce financially. Joyce's thank you, never spoken, was friendly lines about "young Colum" and a mention of Colum's poem, "A Drover," in *Ulysses*. Now Colum could tell his friend of the changes in Ireland, and they could reminisce, as they always did, about the old days, which were their young days, in Dublin.

When they returned to New York, the Colums decided to "move to the country" because of high rents in the city.[38] Elinor Wylie helped them find a house in New Canaan, Connecticut, where they lived very happily for three years, making new friends including Eugene O'Neill and his second wife, Agnes, and the editor Maxwell Perkins who would publish Molly's first book, the critical study, *From These Roots* (1937). Small-town life and commutes to New York City were the background for a very productive period in Colum's life. In the mid and late 1920s he published *The Voyagers* (1925), *The Forge in the Forest* (1925), *The Road Round Ireland* (1926), *Creatures* (1927), and *Orpheus* (1930). Molly was getting regular work for New York newspapers and developing a reputation as a literary critic.

In 1928, missing their friends and the bustle of the city, the Colums moved back to New York. They would continue to spend summers in Connecticut, however, for many years.

All his life after leaving Ireland Colum felt himself to be a frustrated dramatist.[39] He came to realize that he might have been wrong, or at least professionally unwise, to battle Yeats and Lady Gregory. Surely he must have mused if it would not have been a better thing to have remained with the Abbey in Ireland, and thus to have had a continuing opportunity to be a direct part of an historical and cultural dynamic? Trying for Broadway, he wrote *Balloon*, but it never got farther than a 1946 two-week experimental production. Rewritten and produced twice more, it still had no success.

There were compensations. Europe beckoned once more. The Colums enjoyed travel and loved the international life of the between-the-wars literary world. They sailed to Ireland again in the summer of 1929 and next year went over to France in what turned out to be a three-year stay. The friendship between the Colums and the Joyces grew stronger. Padraic, ever the generous friend, actually typed pages of what would become *Finnegans Wake* for Joyce who was nearly blind by this time. On a short trip to Dublin Colum made inquiries for Joyce, who would never return to his native city, about the last days of the novelist's deceased father.[40] And, in Paris again, the Colums became godparents to Joyce's grandson. Also they helped the Joyces with their mentally ill daughter, who came to live with them. [41]

The last time Colum saw Joyce was in the summer of 1939.[42] The novelist, full of troubles, was struggling to finish *Finnegans Wake*. He urged the Colums to return home before the war storm brewing on the European horizon broke and crashed over the civilization they loved. The Colums, Joyce knew, would be safe in America. He died in Zurich in January 1941. Long after the war the Colums received a last letter from Joyce's wife, Nora. She was nearly destitute, beset with illness, and reduced to selling her husband's manuscripts. The letter thanked the Colums for sending her money. It was signed with warmest thanks.[43]

The Depression

However, in 1930 the Colums and the Joyces were flourishing, that is, until the Depression hit them. The publishing business, like most others, went bad. Even though they had just published Colum's collected *Poems* (1932), Macmillan unilaterally decided to terminate their sixteen-year relationship with him. A fighting Irishman would not take that lying down. From Paris, dated 14 July 1932, he replied to H.S. Latham:

Dear Mr. Latham,
    Your letter and telegram mean that the Macmillan Co. are leaving me, an author who has given them twenty books, without any income whatever. And on what pretence? That I have a deficit of 2709 dollars. But this includes 500 dollars advance on *"The Hen Wife's Son"* on which I am working, and part of which I have left in your office, and 500 dollars on *"The First Sparrows"* with an unearned advance on *"Castle Conquer."* These advances can take care of themselves: any publisher in New York would be glad to let me have 1000 dollars on two books and to wait a few years for them. As to *"Castle Conquer,"* by putting it with a collected edition of my work in the near future you will be able to get rid of the copies you have on hand. And you do not take into account the fact that you have two books from me this year—my Collected Poems and my Essays—my Poems which, I venture to say, will be amongst the most steady selling books on your list. Before writing a letter that terminates my income, you should have waited to see how my poems were selling and what prospects my Essays. You have taken for your ruthless accounting the only year in the past ten years in which I have had no book published. I shall not forget that the Macmillan Co. are more anxious to take a stand on their auditors' report rather than on their author's interest. I should like to remind them that publishers live by authors, not by auditors. If their authors get disgusted with them or are forced into other ways of earning a living, what good will their auditors be to them? . . .
    If Macmillans withhold the total earnings on my books, I shall have the matter debated in the literary journals of America and Europe. Some arrangement will have to be made to give me means of living. If you, with twenty books of mine in your possession, refuse to make it, I shall fight you about it before turning to other openings. I know that this is a difficult time for publishers and authors. I do not want to be insistent nor difficult. I pro-

pose that you make me an allowance of one-hundred dollars per month with a thousand dollars advance on my new book, *"Other Roads in Ireland."* If you are willing to do this, cable me on receipt of this letter.[44]

The counter-attack or bluff worked, and Colum was kept on the payroll although with less remuneration. Well, if times were hard for Padraic and Molly, they were hard for everyone else too, and the Colums were as used to financial adversity as any literary couple could be. And life in Europe was cheaper, especially on the French Riviera, where the winter was mild and the conversation grand. They moved to Nice initially because Molly, never the healthiest person, was taken ill and had an operation in Paris. The sunny, breezy Riviera proved to be an ideal place for Colum to write and Molly to convalesce. Macmillan, pleased with Colum's output, even came forward with fresh advances.

Settling in New York City

A fine opportunity, an editorship of the *Forum*, arose for Molly upon her recovery, but it required that they end their idyllic life on the Mediterranean shore and return to New York, where they took up residence in the Beekman Towers Hotel. Now used to wintering in the sun, they managed to obtain winter teaching positions for several years at the University of Miami. While Molly was editing at the *Forum* until the periodical ceased publication in 1940, and also contributing to other distinguished periodicals, Padraic was publishing a book a year until 1940, including poetry, children's books, and folklore.

The Colums decided to try living in Connecticut once more, but the move was ill-fated. Molly was knocked down by a car and seriously injured. Upon her recovery they moved back to New York City, and after living on Claremount Avenue for a while, they settled into an apartment on Central Park West, where they would live until Molly's death in 1957. Padraic would stay on there until a stroke in the summer of 1970 forced a retreat to a nursing home in Enfield, Connecticut.

The Central Park West apartment was near Columbia University, where the Colums received a joint appointment in 1939, team teaching comparative literature until 1956. Colum served as President of

the Poetry Society of America from 1938 to 1939. The next year he
received the Poetry Society of America Medal. *Flower Pieces* appeared
in 1939 and *The Frenzied Prince* in 1943. United States citizenship
came to them through naturalization belatedly in 1945, thirty-one
years after they first arrived in America.

During the 1940s the Colums also managed to teach from time to
time at the University of Wisconsin at Madison and at City College
of New York. Colum modestly avowed that he was not much of a
teacher, that Molly was the real teacher, although he could stir up
some interest in poetry.[45]

Molly's Death

During the late 1940s and much of the 1950s the Colums spent
their summers at the summer residence of a friend, Mrs. Murray
Crane, in Woods Hole on Cape Cod. There Colum would often lecture and give poetry readings. After Molly died, he continued to
summer there. In the 1950s he wrote some of his finer prose. *The
Flying Swans* (1957), his second novel, is the book Colum called his
best.[46] Molly had received a contract to write *Our Friend James Joyce*,
but illness and death intervened and Column finished the book which
came out in 1958.

By far, Colum's most ambitious prose nonfiction was his biography
of his friend, Arthur Griffith. Colum had started work on the book
just after Griffith died in 1922, but he found it very difficult to finish. He knew that Griffith, as a Treaty supporter, would always be
a controversial figure to his generation. Griffith's political friends
were anxious for a laudatory biography, while Colum was reluctant to
get involved in the volatile Irish political scene. Nevertheless, in
1959, with research help from Sean Milroy,[47] financial aid from Irish
millionaire Joseph McGrath, a long stay in Ireland, a massive amount
of information, and a lot of time, Colum published *Ourselves Alone:
Arthur Griffith and the Origins of the Irish Free State.*

Molly's death was a great loss for Colum. Their long marriage had
indeed been a happy partnership. Fortunately for Colum, her
nephew, Emmet Greene, moved in with him after Molly's funeral,
serving as a loyal friend and helper.[48] Greene's support allowed the
poet to undertake a long series of lectures around the country. Ap-
proaching eighty, he remained clear and vigorous. At age eighty-five
he managed a trip to Australia.

Years of Honor

The 1950s and 1960s were years of honor for Padraic Colum. The National University of Ireland awarded him an honorary doctorate in 1951. Colum, remembering his limited formal education, and how he admired the university students, like James Joyce, in his youth, surely was most delighted to be so honored in his native city. The next year he became a fellow of the Academy of American Poets. In 1953, when the second, enlarged edition of his *Collected Poems* was published, he was given the Lady Gregory Award from the Academy of Irish Letters. Both of Colum's countries honored him in 1958 when two of the world's most distinguished universities granted him honorary doctorates: Columbia University and Trinity College, Dublin. In 1961 the Catholic Library Association presented Colum with the Regina Medal. The American Academy of Letters elected him to membership in 1963, and in 1964 Georgetown University awarded him the 175th anniversary Medal of Honor.

Colum's interest in, and writing of, poetry continued into and throughout his last years. *Irish Elegies* first published in 1958, was revised and added to twice, in 1961 and 1966. *The Poet's Circuit* appeared in 1960 and a last book of poetry, *Images of Departure*, was published in 1969, when Colum was nearly eighty-seven years old. New historical plays of his received experimental productions in New York and Dublin in the 1960s, and Colum remained an active writer, a man of letters who had published more than fifty books, up until his stroke in 1970.

Colum died at the Parkway Pavilion in Enfield, Connecticut, on 11 January, 1972, a month after his ninetieth birthday. The body was viewed at the Abbey Funeral Home on Lexington Avenue and 68th Street in Manhattan. A high Mass of the Resurrection was conducted at St. Patrick's Cathedral on Fifth Avenue. Padraic Colum was taken home to Ireland for the last time and interred in St. Fintan Cemetery, Sutton, County Dublin. It was fitting, for he remained true to his credo: "I have identified myself with a particular Irish memory, a particular Irish tradition; it is the memory and the tradition of the historic Irish people."[49]

Chapter Two
Drama: The Promising Start

Padraic Colum's best plays were his first three-act dramas: *Broken Soil* (1903), which was later rewritten as *The Fiddler's House, The Land* (1905), and *Thomas Muskerry* (1910). "These plays," he said, "were conceived in the early days of the Irish National Theatre. I had been one of the group that formed the National Theatre Society and I wrote plays for players who were my colleagues and instructors; I wrote them for a small, barely furnished stage in a small theatre; I wrote them for an audience that was tremendously interested in every expression of national character."[1] On the basis of these dramas and some one-act plays Colum was recognized as one of the most promising dramatists of the Irish Renaissance along with William Butler Yeats, AE (George Russell), Lady Gregory, John Millington Synge, and later Sean O'Casey. He failed to live up to this promise and remained a frustrated, disappointed playwright for some sixty years. Yet his three plays written for the emerging nationalistic drama of Ireland earned him a position in the forefront of the exciting Dublin literary scene at the turn of the century, and some critics thought that he would become the greatest dramatist in Irish history.

As a neophyte playwright he learned part of his craft from the actor-directors William and Frank Fay, who wisely felt that the best way to teach stagecraft to a twenty-year-old dramatist was to put him on the stage as an actor. Also, he learned poetic language from AE and the use of symbol from Yeats; both poets were Colum's mentors. The young writer, still working in the railway clearing house, embraced Yeats's dramatic credo:

A play . . . should contain some criticism of life, founded on the experience or personal observation of the writer, or some vision of life, of Irish life by preference, important from its beauty or from some excellence of style; and this intellectual quality is not more necessary to tragedy than to the gayest comedy.[2]

In 1906, at the age of twenty-four, and with only two full-length plays produced, Colum precociously stated his own concept of a national drama for Ireland, based on his extensive study of Henrik Ibsen. He believed that Irish playwrights "might bring back that eloquence which has been so long out of European literature."[3]

Colum might have been able to make a major contribution to drama, surpassing Synge as the playwright of the Irish peasant world and equaling O'Casey's chronicling of the urban Irish character. Alas, it was not to be. Dilution of energies and purposes, an overwhelming desire to write for an international audience, the rift with the Abbey Company, and ultimately, emigration dissipated Colum's potential for greatness as a dramatist. Even before he left Ireland in 1914, Cornelius Weygandt, the first American critic to study the new Irish drama, wrote of him: "As a dramatist he is still more full of promise than of achievement, and to be a dramatist of promise after ten years of playwrighting is to be at a standstill. In lyric poetry it is otherwise with Mr. Colum. There he has attained. You will find his real value in "Wild Earth" . . . here is imagination, here is lyric cry."[4]

Padraic Colum achieved an early leading position in the new drama of Ireland because of his innovative ability to reproduce peasant speech and values, as well as his skill in selecting plot situations that touched but did not inflame the nerves of the politically sensitive and very literate audience of turn-of-the-century Dublin. Almost alone of the early dramatists, he was a country person and a Roman Catholic. He would later say "Yeats, Lady Gregory, Synge, and all were doing it, but the truth of the matter is that I was the only one of the lot that knew what the real country speech sounded like. . . ."[5]

The Saxon Shillin'

The publication of Colum's one-act play *The Saxon Shillin'* (1902) brought the twenty-year-old clerk to the attention of Yeats and the Fays. The Irish National Theatre Society was to produce the play in January 1903, but the Society withdrew the play ostensibly because it was difficult to stage but probably because Willie Fay feared government reprisal against the fledgling company because of the controversial subject matter. The play was performed by an amateur group, the Daughters of Erin, at the Bamba Hall on 15 May 1903.[6]

The Saxon Shillin' tells the story of Hugh Kearny, a young Irishman, who, as many did, joined the British army for economic reasons. In the course of his service the army expects him to participate
in the eviction of his family and the destruction of their house. When
Kearny learns that his father has been taken prisoner and only his sister remains to guard the house, he picks up his father's old gun and
calling other Irishmen to arms too, goes to his death in defense of his
home.[7]

The play is very powerful; it is Colum's most revolutionary tract.
Willie Fay was quite right in recognizing the inflammatory appeal of
the piece at a time when the nationalistic movement in Ireland was
growing rapidly and many English people were angry at the refusal
of some Irish to support the Boer War and the enlistment of others
on the side of the enemy. Colum's use of Hugh's father's gun as a
symbol of Irish power and the historic call to arms would have landed
the author in prison in almost any other colonial occupation except
the more benign one of the English in Ireland. Colum's moral, suc-
cinctly expressed in the line: "We can't buy ourselves back with the
money we sold ourselves for," perfervidly expressed the historic Irish
dilemma. The words touched the mind and the heart of every Irishman who read them in the *United Irishmen* or heard them from the
stage. Colum was off to a flying start as a dramatist.

Broken Soil and *The Fiddler's House*

Colum almost immediately became a mainstay of the new Irish
National Theatre Society. *Broken Soil* (1903) was his first full-length
contribution to the burgeoning movement. William Fay vividly recalled Colum, the writing of the play, its rapturous reception, and
that Maire Quinn, the actess, had introduced Colum to him.[8]

Broken Soil was revised and retitled for production in 1907. *The
Fiddler's House* is far better organized than the lashed-up earlier version. It is best to use the 1925 revised edition of *Three Plays* in study-
ing Colum's early drama. Whereas the original title denotes the
hero's break with the soil to serve music, the new title indicates
Colum's debt and homage to Ibsen's *A Doll's House*.[9] In both plays
the title character leaves a comfortable home to follow a principle.
Also the character types in *The Fiddler's House* and Colum's other early

plays slowly reveal truths about their social situations and their psychological makeup, much in Ibsen's manner.

The Fiddler's House tells the story of Conn Hourican, a middle-aged peasant fiddler, who is torn between his duty to his children and his land, and his love for music and the road. His love for music almost obliterates his love for his two daughters, Maire and Anne. He neglects his farm, symbolic of Ireland, to pursue his fiddling and his roaming, but Anne, his sturdy Irish daughter, will save the farm. She marries a hard-working young farmer and the future is safe in their hands. Maire is much more complicated a character than her sister. She is both attracted to and repelled by her fiercely masculine horse-taming lover, Brian. Long before D.H. Lawrence did it, Colum depicted male sexual power, fascinating, compelling, and terrifying to a sensitive woman, through the relationship of a man to his proud, strong, beautiful horses, on which he exercises control and wins obedience. Brian is dangerous, wild, almost sinister. He would like to abduct Maire. He seems amoral, especially when he tempts Conn to the tavern causing the older man to break his word to Maire that he would not go. Brian is a character whose moral ambiguity and psychological complexity would fit well into a contemporary plot. Maire leaves Brian to roam with her father on the highways and byways of old Ireland. In the end she meets Brian and, overcoming her sexual fears, permits her doomed father to go on without her, as she prepares to return to her lover.

Although Maire is an extraordinary character, it is Conn who is Colum's triumph. The likeable "Con" artist ("Con" is how the name is spelled in *Broken Soil*) is wonderfully adept at avoiding physical labor. Like many of Synge's and O'Casey's heroes, he is wanting in ambition and concern for his loved ones. Like early twentieth-century Ireland herself, Conn is torn between the easy-going bardic ways of the past, symbolized by his ever-present fiddle, so much like the heraldic harp of yore, and the need to make the land fruitful. Conn says: "Sure the world knows that a man is born with the gift, and isn't the gift then the sign of the grace of God?"[10] It is his credo and his cop-out. In Colum's eyes, Conn, like his countrymen, thirsts for drink and thirsts for life and thirsts for freedom, but cannot reconcile these needs with a devotion to husbandry, stability, and progress.

Besides excellent characterization, Colum also provided his audience with prose that is both an accurate replica of turn-of-the century

Irish Midlands dialect and also lyrical and lovely, as when Conn
expounds:

No man knows how his own life will end; but them that have the gift have
to follow the gift. I'm leaving this house behind me; and maybe the time
will come when I'll be climbing the hills and seeing this little house with
the tears in my eyes. I'm leaving the land behind me too; but what's the
land after all against the music that comes from the far, strange places,
when the night is on the ground and the bird in the grass is quiet? [*Outside
the fiddle is heard again.*] (*TP*, 76)

Conn's philosophy, that of the itinerant artist, expressing the over-
powering need of the artist to follow his music despite the loss and
the pain of departure, could indeed express Colum's own view and
thus foreshadow his later self-exile.[11]

Although *The Fiddler's House* portrays no great historical event, depicts no tragic national hero, nor offers a time-transcending pageant,
it remains a fine national drama because it captures the spirit of the
Irish peasant character, depicting it with mild comic irony, dignified
sadness, and evocative beauty. Thus, Colum was "in many ways the
first of the Irish realists,"[12] dealing with ordinary life and ordinary
people in a profound way.

When writing what he first alluded to as "The Fiddler's Play,"
Colum had the advice of Yeats. The older and famous poet, interest-
ingly enough, did not try to get the younger author to write like
himself. Instead, he encouraged realism and simplicity even though
he personally believed that a more literary national drama was imper-
ative for a re-emerging, but ancient culture. Also Yeats surely was
aware of Colum's limited education and writing experience. On 30
December 1902, writing a most respectful and appreciative letter to
Yeats, Colum described his work on *Broken Soil*. "I have left the Fiddler play over since I read it to you. But I have reconstructed the
whole thing. The plot is quite simple now, I have cut out all literary
matter and am going to avoid the 'literary picturesque'; it will be
three very short acts."[13]

The three major plays written by Colum for the early twentieth-
century Irish theater all have simple plots; they are devoid of literary
rhapsodizing; they are not "folksy-cutesy." Instead they are direct,

straightforward, carefully pruned, simply set, realistic dramas. The Dublin audience knew the qualities of the people of the plays and therefore could not be fooled. Colum not only did not try to fool them, he did not try to impress them with an erudition he did not have nor a literary style that was not his.

The Land

"*The Land* is a bitter comedy, all the more bitter because its author . . . deplored the facts upon which it was based. . . ."[14] It dramatizes the conflict between the generations: the older fights to keep its tiny piece of marginal Irish soil; the younger struggles to escape into the larger world. The scene is set in 1885, after the long "land war," and just after the passage of the Land Purchase Act, a long-awaited and long-needed reform law which provided that the government would advance funds, to be repaid over many years, that would permit Irish peasants to purchase the land they had worked, provided tenant and landlord agreed on the price.

Two sixty-year-old farmers, Murtagh Cosgar and Martin Douras, had battled for the land they had worked and that they deeply loved. Douras had been imprisoned for "the cause." Cosgar had worked his heart out for the land and in the process had driven all his children away, save for one dull-witted daughter, Sally, and one strong, bright, youngest son, Matt. Douras also has two children: a son, Cornelius, who is a talkative but gentle fool, and a daughter, Ellen, who is intelligent, educated, and completely unwilling to live on the land and become a poor farmer's wife. The dramatic balance between the two families is quite neat, allowing Colum to weave a pattern of tension and anxiety without subplot interference or extraneous material.

Ellen and Matt, the hope for Ireland's future, are in love. Matt's grasping father places impediments in their path, and when he finally relents, it is too late. Ellen can't live without the bright lights, the shops, the culture, the crowded streets of American cities, and Matt can't live without her. They go off to the New World. Thus, although the older generation won the land, it was too late. There was an alternative for the young: America. And the best left. The weak, personified by Sally and Cornelius, will remain and inherit.

The bitterest lines of the play are the final ones. The simpleton

Cornelius, excited by the thought that the land is coming to the farmers, and that one day he will own a piece of it says:

Aren't they foolish to be going away like that, father, and we at the mouth of the good times? The men will be coming in soon, and you might say a few words. (*Martin shakes his head*) Indeed you might, father; they'll expect it of you. (*Martin shakes his head. Murtagh and Sally try to restrain him*) "Men of Ballykilduff," you might say, "stay on the land, and you'll be saved body and soul; you'll be saved in the man and in the nation. The nation, men of Ballykilduff, do you every think of it at all? Do you ever think of the Irish nation that is waiting all this time to be born?" (*He becomes more excited; he is seen to be struggling with words*) END OF PLAY (*TP*, 154)

How ironic that the simple-minded son should call for a stay on the land, that he should be sounding the clarion call to the Irish nation that is waiting to be born. In *The Land* as in *The Fiddler's House,* the soil itself, the very land of Ireland, is a character, a silent but living thing demanding to be loved, to be respected, to be cared for. It waits and broods in the background of the characters' lives. It is the prime mover for tragedy, for, like an unrelenting mother or an unforgiving god, it will not be set aside.

The Land is not a thesis play. "It is a cross section of a living society with men and women who are individual through their likenesses, a society in which men do the right thing the wrong way and there is no cut and dried issue."[15] But it is also a society rent by cross-passions that result in waste, broken dreams, and divisions. Everyone suffers loss. Douras loses the daughter who understands him. Cosgar loses the one son worthy of inheriting the land. Matt must stifle his love for the land he truly appreciates and understands more than his father does. Ellen leaves her country and will always feel some guilt. Even Cornelius and Sally lose as they gain. They lose the future counsel and care of the wise and the good. Thus, although *The Land* is no tragedy of blood and violence and death, nevertheless, the mood is tragic indeed. In the plain tale lies the tragedy of people. No wonder Colum was later able to say that *The Land* was "the first popular success the Abbey Theatre had had."[16]

Published in *Studies* (1907), *The Miracle of the Corn,* a verse play, was first presented on 22 May 1908 by the Theatre of Ireland, which rented the Abbey for the occasion.[17] As a play, the work was not and is not a success. It is too heavily symbolic, too imitative of Yeats.

Colum's simple plot, essentially an allegory or an Irish morality play, cannot sustain the massive religious metaphor. The allegorized action is deadly. The obvious literary structure breaks through the fabric of the play, as the charitable wife of a rich farmer gives her husband's grain (*corn* in British English) to the poor and, consequently, the farmer's supply increases and he grows even more wealthy. Thus, she becomes a fertility symbol and also a Virgin Mother providing a miracle of plenty. Colum made the mistake of breaking with his own dramaturgical rules and deviating from what he wrote best: realistic Irish peasant drama. He quickly returned to strength in his next play.

Thomas Muskerry

Padraic Colum's last major dramatic contribution to the Abbey Theatre movement was also his most controversial play, both as a piece of provocative dramatic literature and in the circumstances surrounding its initial Dublin run. *Thomas Muskerry* was scheduled to be performed at the Abbey Theatre on 5, 6, 7 May 1910. The director was to be Lennox Robinson, who later wrote to Yeats:

> You have asked me to tell you exactly what happened on May 7th last. I read in the morning papers of the King's death, but I never thought of the effect it would have on the theatres and places of amusement. However about 11.15 our secretary came to my rooms and told me that he heard that the other theatres in Dublin were closing and asked me what we should do. I knew that the Abbey Theatre had been carried on from the beginning as a purely artistic venture, I knew that its policy was to ignore politics, and I thought that if we closed we would be throwing ourselves definitely on one political side and that we should remain open taking no notice of a circumstance that had no significance to the arts. However I decided to leave the matter to Lady Gregory and wired to her as follows:
>
> > "Theatres closing here. What am I to do? I think we should remain open but leave decision to you."

This was handed in ten minutes before twelve. I then went to the Theatre and waited for a reply; none came, and I decided to go on with the matinee. Lady Gregory's answer desiring the Theatre to be closed came in the course of the afternoon—in the interval before the last act of the play we were performing.

"Should close through courtesy. A. Gregory."

It was too late to stop the matinee then, and the good audience encouraged me to think that little criticism would be passed on our having remained open. It was too late to put notices in the evening papers cancelling the night performances and if there was any crime in having played we had already committed it."[18]

The Abbey's financial backer, Miss Elizabeth Horniman, an Englishwoman, reacted to the performance of *Thomas Muskerry* immediately and emphatically. She wired to Lady Gregory: "Opening last Saturday was disgraceful. Performance on day of funeral would be political and would stop subsidy automatically."[19] Miss Horniman also demanded a public apology. The theater company offered a halfhearted one and Miss Horniman withdrew her support.[20] Fortunately the Abbey survived.

Thomas Muskerry also provoked another donnybrook, a battle of critics. No one was indifferent to the play. The ardent nationalists, the same people who had attacked Synge's *Playboy of the Western World* for its realistic portrayal of Irish peasant life, now went after Colum for defaming the Irish character. Other, more objective reviewers greatly admired the play and even called him the successor to Ibsen as a realist writer. The skirmishing continued for three years. *Sinn Fein,* the nationalistic periodical, published a series of articles called "Muskerryism" which both praised and damned the author: praised him for his Ibsen-like realism and damned him for his supposed pandering to an English audience.[21] The latter charge particularly enraged Colum. He replied:

I have never written an Irish play for an English audience. *Thomas Muskerry* was written for an Irish audience. It was produced in London as it might have been produced in the Shetland Islands. I did not spend twopence in discovering what the London papers wrote about my play. In connection with the London production the document that had the most interest for me was the royalty account. I have given my play to an Irish theatre. They are at liberty to produce it in London, New York, or Paris. . . .

I assure you . . . that any play written by me for a non-Irish theatre will have no connection with Ireland.[22]

Colum remained true to his word, with unfortunate results, until the 1960s. His future plays were either devoid of the Irish content necessary to his art, or because he eventually lost touch with the soil of Ireland, they were lacking in authenticity.

His working title for *Thomas Muskerry* was "The Workhouse Master," obviously a more descriptive title. However, Colum changed the title to the protagonist's name upon the request of Lady Gregory, who had written *The Workhouse Ward*. It was thought best to end possible confusion between two plays.

Thomas Muskerry is not a play set in the Irish countryside and rooted in the soil of Ireland, the ancient place Colum knew from his grandparents and which he portrays in *The Fiddler's House* and *The Land*. Instead this drama is set in small-town society and the institution of the workhouse, places he knew from his uncle and his father. It is the intriguing, conniving, grasping, mean world of the nineteenth-century petite bourgeoisie "where the poorest of the paupers and the simple-minded Muskerry himself are its only decent characters. . . . In Colum's plays, country-men, faithfully and without prejudice as they are revealed, are a finer and more vital group than its people of the small towns: here, as elsewhere, apparently, if God made the country and man made the town, the devil made the country-town."[23]

The play is a Balzac-like, unrelenting study of humankind's meanness and ingratitude. Thomas Muskerry is the sixty-year-old master of the Garrisowen Workhouse in the Irish Midlands. He is a decent, basically compassionate, somewhat vain and self-congratulating man, who has circumscribed his life with conventions, habit, and petty and brief authority. Like King Lear, he is sure of his position and has provided for his old age through a promised pension with which he will live in a small cottage on the land, where he will be respected by his daughter and her family with whom he has been generous, and where also he expects the world will continue to respect him and defer to him as "the master." Little moves him from his complacency except when the dignified figure of the blind piper, Myles Gorman, relates how his brother robbed him of his land, but in doing so inadvertently gave him the freedom of the road.

As in Greek tragedy, it is soon clear that fate has other plans for Thomas Muskerry. He begins the classic, intersecting fall and rise of tragedy. He suffers, but his soul rises and his wisdom and understanding grow, despite and because of his inevitable downfall. His daughter and her unsuccessful shopkeeper husband force him to retire, steal his substance, destroy his dream of a country house, and, in the end, shut him up in the workhouse he once administered, where God takes him in a pauper's bed. His only companion is its old, blind piper:

MUSKERRY: Myles—Myles Gorman—come back.

GORMAN: What will I do for you, Master?

MUSKERRY: Say a prayer for me.

GORMAN: What prayer will I say, Master?

MUSKERRY: Say "God be good to Thomas Muskerry."

GORMAN: [*taking off his hat*] "God be good to Thomas Muskerry, the man who was good to the poor." Is that all, Master?

MUSKERRY: That's—that's all.

[*Gorman goes to the door.*]

GORMAN: In a little while you'll hear my pipes on the road. [*He goes out. There is the sound of heavy breathing from the bed. Then silence.*] (TP, 238)

Thomas Muskerry, unlike Colum's other plays, contains no humor. Like all true tragedy, it is devoid of poetic justice except that the viewer realizes that Muskerry's daughter, Mrs. Crilly, will be treated just as badly by her daughter, Anna, and her son, Albert, in good time. Thus, even the younger generation cannot be admired in the play. Anna refuses to part with her dowry after her father has lost all but it in a stupid business deal. It is her new husband, James Scollard, now the workhouse's master, who prevents Muskerry from leaving to go to his new home in the country, because his mother-in-law insists that the town would not like the idea of her father living alone and not in her house, thus negatively affecting business in the grocery shop. All of the principals of Muskerry's life share a portion of sin: the deadly sin of greed. Cannibal-like they feed on the living.

Muskerry is one of Colum's finest dramatic characters. Like King Lear, he is betrayed by his own family. Like King Lear, he has a loyal supporter: the old, blind piper. Like King Lear, he is tortured by and must endure the insolence of a servant, Felix Tournour. And like King Lear, he comes to transcend his suffering and to reinherit his dignity as a human being. The play ends with a sense of loss that is reminiscent of Shakespearean tragedy. The world is a meaner place, a lesser place, a sphere without dignity, purpose, and order, with old Thomas Muskerry gone.

Although the plot creaks along somewhat predictably, the other characters of the play are almost as well drawn as the hero. Mrs. Crilly is a study of banal evil worthy of Goneril or Regan. Her inept, heavy-drinking spouse, is thoroughly and believably despicable. The children are truly the scions of their parents. Myles Gorman, blind like Tiresias, stands and watches and plays chorus to and recorder of the small-scale tragedy of Thomas Muskerry. Gorman personifies the spirit of art and the spirit of Ireland. He is the author's surrogate. Through him we come to understand that Thomas Muskerry stands for the loss of peasant virtues in his "indirect contact with the ambitions and practices of urban civilization."[24]

Colum, even in his youth, showed great sympathy for and understanding of old age. Like Shakespeare, he knew that it could promote great evil in ordinary, unfeeling, mean-spirited people, even when they are related to the old. He understood that financial loss is not the great terror of the aged. Each fears, as Muskerry says, "The loss of my trust, the loss of my dignity, my self-respect. . . ." (*TP*, 213). Each dreads the murder of the spirit. Colum said, "the tragedy of the play is due to the impotence of old age."[25] It is more, it is the very vulnerability of life, surely not only in old Ireland but everywhere and always. For life without any reserve must always be life on the edge.

The Contribution to Irish Renaissance Drama

Padraic Colum's early plays had an important effect on both the drama of Ireland and the drama of England. Due to the verisimilitude of his language a flood of "peasant plays" followed hard upon *Broken Soil* and *The Land*.[26] Native dialects and customs were from his time on frequently and seriously presented on the Irish stage. Never again would stilted stage English appear in realistic Irish drama, purporting to be native speech.

Colum's later summation of the contribution of the Abbey Theatre Movement must include his own contribution: "We can now ask what the movement that created the Abbey Theatre has actually accomplished. Briefly stated, it has produced a national drama for Ireland; it has intensified in Irish writers national characteristics, and it has encouraged them to write plays that are charged with Irish temperament, the Irish instincts, the Irish tradition."[27]

As to an influence on the drama of England, Colum's brilliant if intuitive grasp of the poetry inherent in the peasant prose of Irish-English helped make possible and true Una Ellis-Fermor's statement: "It was left to the Irish Dramatic Movement to bring back to the English theatre the poetry that it had missed in Ibsen, presenting it, if not in terms of English society at least in a language which Englishmen could understand, and not leaving it to them to make either translations or selections."[28]

Years of Frustration

Many critics believe that Padraic Colum ended his career as a playwright with the production of *Thomas Muskerry* in 1910. L. A. G. Strong, the most ardent advocate of Colum's poetry, stated: "I am passing by the plays, accepting Colum's own unspoken comment on them, the fact that he so soon decided to leave the stage alone."[29] In truth, Colum never left the stage alone; in a very real sense the stage left him alone. All his life after 1910, in Ireland, in America, in England, he continued to write and rewrite plays (mostly rewrite), and he struggled, manipulated, cajoled, plotted, and nearly begged, almost always unsuccessfully, for productions of new or revised work. In 1969 he said to an interviewer: "I am primarily a man of the theatre and have always been. . . . If I am not a playwright, I am nothing."[30] Although new plays after *Thomas Muskerry* were relatively few, revision of older plays, especially *The Desert*, which he first completed in 1907, consumed much of his creative energy.

From 1910 through the early 1960s Colum wrote two one-act plays, *The Destruction of the Hostel* (1910), *The Betrayal* (1914); two full-length plays: "Theodora of Byzantium" (1912) and *Balloon* (1926–1929); and five short plays about Irish history based on the Japanese Noh dramas as introduced to English-language drama by Yeats in 1915: *Moytura, Glendalough, Cloughoughter, Monasterboice,* and *Kilmore* (1961–1966). However, he also adapted quite a few plays for the stage, including *Grasshopper* (1917) based on his and F.E. Washburn Freund's adaptation of *Ein Frühlingsopper* (1903) by Herman Keyserling, which Colum recast as an Irish peasant play, and which was produced in London and New York (Colum's only Broadway production) in 1917 and then at the Abbey in 1922, where the text was later lost in a fire;[31] a version of the English Cycle Play, *The Second Shepherd's Play* (1917), which Colum said Yeats had asked him to write; *The Show Booth* (1921); *Hansel and Gretel*(1952), a scenario for a motion-picture puppet cartoon; *Ulysses in Nighttown* (1958), a successful off-Broadway adaptation of James Joyce's novel; and *Carricknahauna* (1967), a less successful adaptation of Colum's poetry, also presented off-Broadway.

Thus, it is clear that Colum never lost interest and involvement in the theater. Yet three things went wrong with his playwriting. First of all, the move to America effectively cut off his roots to the Irish peasantry, and the frequent visits after World War I could not renew them. Second, the lost connection with the Abbey Theatre was debilitating. Colum needed the discipline of a production schedule and collective company advice and consent to produce first-class work. Third, he became intrigued with experimentation and historic fantasy, especially after he began to write books for children. His developing imagination worked exceedingly well for children's literature, but was deadly for his drama and it destroyed him as a realistic playwright.

Later Plays

Padraic Colum worked on *The Desert* for almost fifty years. Beginning in 1907 Colum believed that his simple folk tale of a beggar who wanders in from the desert, nearly becomes a vizier or king, and in the end returns to the desert in his original state, could be the stuff of epic and spectacular theater provided it had an exotic enough setting. He was dead wrong. The first production as *Mogu the Wanderer* with Orson Welles as the King of Persia at Dublin's Gate Theatre on 29 December 1931 and 7 January 1932 was a failure. The audience and even the actors laughed at the pretentiousness of the play and the absurdity of the situation.

However, Colum never gave up on the play. It underwent many changes. He wrote at least four full-length versions set in such diverse places as North Africa, the Roman City of Baalbek in Lebanon, Persepolis in Persia, and Islamic West Africa. The titles reflect the changing locales: *The Desert, Mogu the Wanderer,* "The Vizier" and "Timbuktu." The first and last version do not share one line of dialogue and almost every character is different.

The Desert was a creative disaster for Colum. He was deluded about his importance, but, most of all, he believed that the playwright Edward Knoblock had stolen the idea and setting of *The Desert,* having

either read the manuscript in London or having been told the plot by
a theater manager to whom Colum had sent the script. The fiery
young Irishman was sure that Knoblock's *Kismet* was a plagiarized
version of his play, and he spent much time and effort trying to obtain redress. He was unsuccessful and, indeed, probably wrong. As a
result, he was convinced that *The Desert* could and should be as popular and successful as *Kismet.* It never happened.

"Theodora of Byzantium," first written in 1912, was Colum's second non-Irish play and the last full-length drama he would attempt
while still residing in his native land. Like *The Desert,* he kept revis-
ing it up to 1957, although it was never produced or published. The
play's last title is the improbable "The Bear Keeper's Daughter." It
is partially in verse and is based on the historian Procopius's history
of the Byzantine empress and emperor Theodora and Justinian.
"Theodora" is Colum's only attempt at the history play.

Theodora is a complex woman. The daughter of a Cyprian bear
keeper, she grows up in a traveling circus. After her father dies, she
is forced to beg to survive. Then she becomes an actress and has many
lovers. Her true love is murdered and she joins pagan rites to obtain
visions of her dead lover. Digusted with her life, she returns to Con-
stantinople where Justinian discovers her as a charitable Christian
woman. Very complicated actions ensue: a plot to overthrow Justinian is thwarted, Theodora reverts to pagan ritual to discover the
murderer of her former lover and has him murdered, and Theodora
uses her acting ability to aid Justinian. At the end Theodora is grand,
majestic, and very human; a woman finally freed from the excessive
passion of her youth.

The character of Theodora is thus well drawn, but this is not
enough to carry the play. The plot is too complicated and the rest of
the characters are made of cardboard. Colum's technique as a playwright was to revise continuously, building up a play until he was
satisfied with it. "Theodora of Byzantium" ended as a jerry-built
structure.[32]

Colum's most frequently produced play is *The Betrayal,* a one-act,
revolutionary drama that the Abbey Theatre felt was too inflammatory to produce and the London Theatre also found politically unac-
ceptable. Yet the play has been performed in Dublin, New York, and
even Jerusalem. Although set in eighteenth-century Ireland, the
drama is surely applicable to countries today that have or have had
underground resistance movements.[33] In the play the British author-

ities, represented by two brothers, Morgan and Gideon Lefroy, attempt to obtain a reward for the names of those Irishmen who assassinated a British army sergeant. The brothers haggle over the money they have not as yet obtained. Gideon comes up with the idea to get someone in the crowd below his room to seem to betray the killers, thus provoking exposure and retribution. Peg, the Ballad Singer, goes to Morgan Lefroy to ask him to intercede with the British colonel to save her son who has been condemned as a deserter. Peg is mistakenly seen by the people as a betrayer of the cause. She picks up a dagger from a table and stabs Morgan. The crowd below sees the action and she is vindicated. It then turns out, ironically, that her son has betrayed the people to save his own life. Colum thus contrasts the two generations of Irish. The older generation is willing to sacrifice everything for the cause of Irish freedom, while the younger, selfish generation is only concerned with its personal survival. Like *The Saxon Shillin'*, *The Betrayal* is a call to arms against colonialism, exploitation, and tyranny. It completely captured the growing anger of many Irish people two years before the Easter Rebellion of 1916. The character of Peg is yet another strong Irish mother, full of courage, and symbolic of the nation itself.

Balloon (1929) was Colum's last attempt to write a non-Irish play with a fairy-tale or historical motif. Only one version was published, by Macmillan, in 1929, although Colum naturally revised it over the years. On 12 August 1946 the play was finally produced at the Ogunquit Playhouse in Maine, where it had a successful two-week run. Colum fervently hoped for a Broadway production. But he later said, "And then after I had imagined myself as making money on Broadway it never went on. The usual disappointment. So I am a foiled, frustrated dramatist."[34]

The play is a four-act, symbolic-surrealistic quest for both a definition of the hero in modern society and for a return to a simple, natural world, brought about by a rejection of materialistic values. *Balloon* is set in and near the Hotel Daedelus in "Metropolis," a cosmopolitan, but superficial and artificial hotel, the name of which is one of several echoes of James Joyce's *A Portrait of the Artist as a Young Man*. The play's title refers to the balloon perched on the hotel roof, in which celebrities are scheduled to make an ascent as a publicity stunt.

At the opening of the play, the protagonist, Caspar, is earning his living tending a telescope in the park near the hotel. He is fond of saying of the moon in his telescope: "Mountain, Extinct Volcanoes, Empty Seas!" as if to imply that those features of the universe are reality whereas the hotel and even human life are momentary phenomena. Yet Caspar longs for mortal fame and for a taste of the luxurious and "significant" life in the hotel.[35]

Caspar confuses fame with notoriety. To his great joy, the hotel's architect buys his telescope for a very generous sum in order to allow Caspar to sample life in the hotel. He says, "A man can become a hero by doing heroic things" (B, 18–19). In the course of the drama Caspar finds his true love, Paros Veba, an Irish-American-Polish girl seeking a husband as, Colum implies, a good Irish-American-Polish girl should; and Caspar comes to learn, after several adventures, that: "One is what one has done, and one is nothing else" (B, 111).

Caspar, and perhaps Colum, defines the hero as the person who is equal to an event and can submerge himself or herself totally in the action of the event. Like Stephen Dedalus in *A Portrait of the Artist as a Young Man,* Caspar is a young man in search of truth and reality and, through these concepts, his own self.

Colum has yet another choruslike musician in *Balloon.* This time his name is Glock and he is an old piper who longs nostalgically for the simple ways of the world past. He still loves nature and is able to return to the countryside as perhaps the poet Colum would have liked.

But the play is weakened by the improbable, fairy-tale-like plot; by the unbelievable characters, many of whom are obvious stereotypes; by having grown through apparent accretions and additions to become overly long; by an allegory—the quest for the return to the simple, natural world through a rejection of materialism—that breaks through the thin fabric of the plot; and by a novelty that transforms simplicity to childishness. It was just as well that in the end Colum returned to familiar Irish themes and left fairy-tale fantasy to his successful career as a writer of children's books.

Final Dramatic Effort: The Noh Plays

In the end it was back to Irish themes. Colum's last efforts in the drama were an attempt to dramatize significant moments in Irish political, military, and cultural history through the Japanese Noh drama tradition, which Yeats had introduced to Western drama some

fifty years before. While still engaged in the writing of his Noh
plays, Colum explained his reasons and methods:

> . . . I've attempted to modify the form of the Noh play. Yeats had done
> it before for the Irish Theatre you know. But his contained purely legendary
> characters. My innovations were historical characters . . . First of all its a
> play that has [its setting] at a shrine or place where some extraordinary event
> happened . . . you can have changes in times. I think that everybody's seek-
> ing for a new form for the theatre. . . . How do you get poetry in? How do
> you get spiritual life? That's the problem. It has been tried in many ways.
> They all tried to get away from the naturalistic thing. [I attempted to take]
> the Japanese form and use it in a new way, the ritual, the sound, and so on
> . . . They are poetry. They give me a better chance to combine poetry with
> drama. . . .[36]

Noh plays make enormous demands on their audiences. They re-
quire strict attention and the ability to comprehend poetic and stylized action presented on several historical levels simultaneously. The
Noh is not essentially storytelling. Instead, it attempts, through ret-
rospection, to invoke an emotional state or create a specific mood.
Verse and prose are combined, and recitation, too, is highly stylized.
A traditional program is made up of five types of plays: a play praising the gods, a play about warriors, a play about women, a play
about a living man, and a play of ghosts. Roles are few; costumes are
rich; settings simple. Noh is the most carefully controlled theater in
the world.

Like the Japanese, Colum's Noh plays are a cycle of five. Also like
the Japanese, Colum's contain both poetry and prose. Since his Noh
plays are about Irish heroes, legends, mythology, and historical
places, they allowed the writer essentially to continue his work as
poet and folklorist, while providing him with the opportunity to ex-
ercise his dramatic talents and yearnings. The 1950s and 1960s were
an era in which Western drama moved away from the realism and
naturalism of modern drama and the strictures of the earlier Ibsenites.
This movement is best illustrated by the popular works of Absurdist–
Existentialist writers like Eugene Ionesco and Samuel Beckett.
Colum's Noh plays, written when they were, are somewhat of a conservative answer to the Absurdist–Existentialists. They are exotic in
setting, nonrealistic in form, yet they are filled with historical per-

sons and settings, and at their best they are beautiful dramatic poems.

The Noh plays, *Moytura,* "Glendalough," "Cloughoughter," "Monasterboice," and "Kilmore" (1961–1966) are all one-acters. Only the first has been published.[37] Three of them, "Monasterboice," "Glendalough," and "Cloughoughter" were grouped together, called "The Challengers," and performed at the Lantern Theatre in Dublin in 1966. The plays have also received radio productions.[38]

Moytura is set at the site of a prehistoric battle between the force of light and skill on one side and the opposing force of darkness and destruction. There the ghost of Sir William Wilde, father of Oscar Wilde, in life a well-known surgeon and antiquarian who had both of the forces in him, relives his agony at the news that his two disowned, illegitimate daughters have burned to death in an accident. Wilde's connection with Moytura is that the doctor excavated the site and built his house there. He named his house Moytura.

As Wilde's emotions rise upon rehearing the sad news, two chorus figures relate the feelings and passions of ancient warriors. Wilde speaks to Nuada, an ancient Irish monarch, who gives him strength and comfort. Now he can deal with the guilt that plagues him even in death. In the epilogue yet another chorus figure, a young man, returns to offer history's judgment on Wilde who was exonerated by the court but condemned by the people. Colum successfully merges various historical stages in *Moytura,* implying that history is not only a continuum, but also an echo and a memory. It lives in ancient places, merging with and influencing the present.

"Glendalough" is the first play in the three-drama Challengers series. The challenge is leadership, even when the people served betray the leader, as they always seem to do in Colum's Noh drama. The leader and protagonist in "Glendalough" is the Irish statesman Charles Stuart Parnell, who in the 1880s was leading the Irish nation to Home Rule through his able dealings with and in the British Parliament in London. In 1899, the year of the setting of "Glendalough," the husband of Parnell's mistress, Kathleen (Kitty) O'Shea, sued her for divorce on the grounds of adultery and named Parnell, who would later marry her, as corespondent in the suit. The trial was a major scandal and it destroyed Parnell, his work, and the hope of Home Rule.

In the play Parnell, after the divorce and before a meeting that will determine his fate as an Irish politician, comes to Glendalough, the site of a sixth-century monastery in County Wicklow and the location of a medieval university, where he hopes to undergo self-revelation. The play relates the events leading to his fall: helping Captain O'Shea to become a member of Parliament, his prideful refusal of ministerial aid, and the Catholic church's vehement reaction to the divorce trial, which led to his alienation from the Irish people.

Parnell comes to face his mistakes and his dishonesty. Finally, he realizes that lust has undone him. This revelation is due to the fact that he sees the parallel between his own action and that of St. Kevin, whose church was at Glendalough, and who resisted the sexual temptation of the hag, Kathleen. In self-knowledge is redemption. The play ends with the ghost of a forger, Richard Pigott, rising up to remind Parnell of the forger within himself. But Parnell realizes that eventually the Irish people will vindicate his honor, forgive his weakness, and revere his memory for the good he did and the vision he strove for.

"Cloughoughter" is concerned with a point of decision in the life of Colum's friend, the revolutionary martyr Roger Casement, who was executed by the British on 3 August 1916. Cloughoughter itself is the site of the death on 10 November 1649 of the Irish general, Owen Roe O'Neill, of the great warrior clan, who as a young man had fought in the battle of Kinsale in 1602 where his uncle, Hugh O'Neill, was defeated by Mountjoy, leader of Queen Elizabeth I's army of occupation.

Casement has come to Cloughoughter to determine if he should become the leader of the Irish revolution. Owen Roe O'Neill and two veterans of the battle of Kinsale help Casement to decide to accept the role of leader. The fame that has eluded Owen Roe O'Neill is won by Casement as the audience learns from a ballad heard by Casement's brother at Cloughoughter after the hero's execution.

The play is very hard to follow because it exists on four time levels: the early years of the twentieth century preceding Casement's death, Owen O'Neill's time, the battle of Kinsale, and the period immediately after Casement's death in 1916. Also adding to the difficulty is the fact that there are two separate choruses. The multi-time levels and chorus, although a part of the Noh tradition, are cumbersome in "Cloughoughter," particularly for a reader or playgoer not fully familiar with Irish history. The heart of the play, Casement's communing with O'Neill and his pledge to go on to give his life for Ireland's honor, as well as Colum's elegy for Casement, are fine examples of Colum's mature work.

"Monasterboice" is concerned with several problems central to the life and works of Colum's great literary friend James Joyce as well as with Joyce's search for identity as an artist. Although not a military man, Joyce is nevertheless a hero for Colum, a hero of culture whose battleground is the artist's self and whose struggle is with the spiritual, cultural, and temporal powers of the Roman Catholic Church, from which powerful Jesuitical voices call Joyce back to belief, tradition, and obedience.

The play is set in the ancient monastery of Monasterboice, founded in the sixth century, where the great stone Celtic cross within a circle symbolizes the oneness of time that faith provides. Joyce is accompanied there by Erma Clery, who is E.C. in *Portrait of the Artist as a Young Man,* and who has her full name in the earlier work, *Stephen Hero.* She is the siren voice luring the Ulysses-like author to the rocks and shoals of respectable middle-class marriage, conformity, and acceptance. He rejects that siren call and also the appeal of a celibate life in the clergy. In the end, on the way to exile and greatness, Joyce goes off with his father and an old friend to have a "jollification."

"Monasterboice" is weakened by its lack of action. Although Joyce's views of the church, the Irish people, marriage, Parnell's betrayal, art, and history are, of course, very interesting, they are better learned in Joyce's own prose. Without legend, without historical events, and without climax or resolution, the play plods along on an undistinguished realistic level.

"Kilmore," Colum's final drama, deals with the painful decision of Henry Joe McCracken, the Ulster leader, to continue the plans for the ill-fated rising of 1798 in the hope of uniting Catholic and Protestant Ireland, even though he knew that the promised support of the French would not be forthcoming and that the revolt was doomed even before it began. McCracken's indecision, his near-betrayal of the Irish cause, and his final commitment are the conflict and the heart of the play. "Kilmore" is the most realistic of Colum's Noh plays, and it offers the best theater possibilities.

As has been shown, Colum's Noh plays are different from one another, "Kilmore" being the least Noh-like. They show the continuity of Irish history and the relationship of the past to the present. They are about the anguish of leadership and the frailty of even the great and the powerful. They value perseverance and strength of character, so that even a tragic flaw may be overcome by courage and determination. They are finer dramas than all of Colum's plays except for the three at the beginning of his dramatic career. Now his plays are a part of history rather than a part of the living stage. Still his influence was significant in his time, and his work as dramatist throughout his writing career lent dramatic effect to his poetry.

Finally, Colum early on said: "As the dramatist, so are his creations. They are like his time, place, and people. For the sake of more vital expression he is compelled to think in terms of the lives he knows. If he aims at verisimilitude he can write with exactness of manners, customs and characters that he knows intimately. He observes life because he is curious about it."[39]

When Padraic Colum thought in terms of the lives he knew, he was a powerful, creative dramatist. When he forgot his own dictum, his work was wanting.

Chapter Three
The Poet in Ireland: 1902–1914

It was that fascinating poet, mystic, and mentor of young writers, AE (George Russell) who counseled and promoted the young poet, Padraic Colum. Richard Fallis says: "AE's greatest service to Irish literature . . . came neither in his poetry nor his ideas. It came, instead, in his unceasing kindness to young writers. . . . he was, as Frank O'Connor said, the father of three generations of Irish poets. Among his 'discoveries' were James Joyce, Padraic Colum, James Stephens, Frank O'Connor. . . . AE's genius was for dealing with writers at the very beginning of their careers, and often, as they matured, their allegiances turned from him to Yeats."[1] In 1904 AE sponsored *New Songs,* a collection of poems by new, young Irish writers. Some of the writers, representing a fresh vitality in Irish letters, turned away from the subjects and the rhythms of the previous movement, the Celtic Twilight of the 1890s, and combined their own experiences with the folk songs and the situations of the peasants and artisans of the countryside.

Although Colum had published poems in the *United Irishman* and elsewhere before his appearance in *New Songs,* it was the latter publication, containing "The Plougher," "The Bells," "A Drover," and "A Poor Scholar," that confirmed Colum, at age twenty-three, as an important figure in the heady Dublin literary scene. From the beginning, Colum believed that he had a mission as a poet. He would express the fundamental nature and the "common furniture" of Irish daily life. In this service he intended to spend his life, partly in creating for himself the Walt Whitman-like aura of people's poet. In Whitman's case the character created was that of the worker poet; Colum chose the peasant bard as his persona. Although he would live most of his life in New York City and environs, and could often be found in Dublin or London or Paris or even on the Riviera, he nevertheless cultivated the look, manner, dialect, joviality, and gentle earthy wisdom of an Irish village poet, writing sentimental verse more native to the folk song, but never crossing the critical line to self-parody or meretricious entertainment.[2] Like Whitman, lacking in formal education, he chose, as the child does, to sing of the simple things.

Colum was fortunate that the early events of his life brought him to Dublin, where, as he would later say, "there was always a poet ready to deliver the lyric he had just written to another poet, ready to listen to another, to comment on what the other had done. It is the comment made in this way that really teaches the young poet: it is from his contemporaries he learns technique and receives ideas."[3] But Colum, if he were to achieve his dream of becoming the national poet of Ireland, needed to model his verse at least in part on the poetry of earlier national poets. He chose Thomas Moore, Sir Samuel Ferguson, and James Clarence Mangan for study.

In Thomas Moore (1779–1852) Colum found inspiration for writing delicate lyric poetry that, although written in English, still contained Irish linguistic patterns and Irish countryside subjects. Colum's mother had loved Moore's *Irish Melodies* (1808) and had often read or sung the poems to her children. Colum hoped that some of his own poems would become part of the "anonymous" folk-song tradition of Ireland as many of Moore's had, and they did.

In Sir Samuel Ferguson (1810–1886), poet and antiquarian, Colum found a model for his attempt, especially in his children's poems, books, and his lost plays, to revivify Ireland's heroic age, as Ferguson had tried to do through epic and folk poetry in *Lays of the Western Gael* (1865) and *Congol* (1872). Not surprisingly, Colum, in his *Anthology of Irish Verse* (1922, revised 1948), credits Moore and Ferguson as the grandfathers of modern Anglo-Irish national poetry, the inspirers of the generation of Yeats.[4]

James Clarence Mangan (1803–1849), Colum said, provided for "the Irish poet who must write in English . . . a form that is distinctly Gaelic."[5] Mangan's poetry follows the syllabic or quantitative discipline of Old and Middle Irish verse rather than the accented meters of English poetry. Mangan emphasized rhyme and alliteration as would Colum. Colum also followed Mangan's lead in directly imposing Gaelic constructions on an English vocabulary.

Prosody

All his artistic life Colum was a careful craftsman of traditional verse, primarily noted for its lyric quality. He almost always employed careful meter and rhyme. He frequently used the ballad stanza and refrain line. Although freer when using the iambic foot, he was extremely regular in his heavy use of the anapest. The heavily stressed, three-beat measure provided a desired songlike quality. To achieve this quality Colum placed "greater emphasis upon sound patterns than English poets ordinarily would. . . ."[6] Thus, Irish sound and traditional forms serve along with peasant dialogue and photographic descriptiveness, as the architectonic of Colum's poetry.

New Songs (1904)

AE placed five poems by Padraic Colum in New Songs, a collection he believed "revealed a new mood in Irish verse."[7] Three of them, "A Portrait" (later titled "A Poor Scholar of the 'Forties,"), "The Plougher," and "A Drover" became "classics" of Colum's canon. "The Plougher" inspired the artist Jack B. Yeats to produce a woodcut, with the same title, which AE selected for New Songs' frontispiece. "A Portrait" is a particularly striking poem, depicting the difficult life of the scholar-teacher of the last century, teaching by a dim rushlight. In smoky cabins, nights and weekends, they taught and the teacher's only reward was that one day he might hear

> Years hence in rustic speech, a phrase,
> As in wild earth a Grecian vase.

The goal of a lifetime, this is modest indeed, perhaps too modest.

This poem, the last line of which would provide the title, Wild Earth, for Colum's first book of poetry, expresses the loneliness of the itinerant teacher in the last century and the near futility of hedgerow schoolmastering. It both extols and deplores the minimal survival of classical culture among the Irish. As in Colum's verse itself, the reader "finds no renaissance, no reflowering of the literary glories of Greece and Rome, but only vestigial remnants of a lost heritage. . . . Nor should one expect to find more. Colum's first loyalty is to the popular tradition."[8]

"The Plougher" may be Colum's best-known poem. It is a subtle, understated poem to the glory of the peasant farmer who in the failing light, perhaps the failing light of civilization, does his daily work. This individual man represents the hope of humankind.

> Slowly the darkness falls, the broken lands
>   blend with the savage,
> The brute-tamer stands by the brutes, by a
>   head's breadth only above them!
>
> A head's breadth, ay, but therein is Hell's depth
>   and the height up to Heaven,
> And the thrones of the gods, and their halls
>   and their chariots, purples and splendours.

Written in hexameters, the poem emits a primitive spirit. The lone farmer, only a little above his animals in the great chain of being, nevertheless is able to break the earth and tame the brutes of nature. Although he may reside on the bottom rung of the ladder of culture, his mind can create heaven and hell and all that imagination is capable of. His great strength lies in the fact that he stands in the earth. Nature communicates; he listens. He has roots. He is a root.

"A Drover" is both a ballad and a dramatic monologue in the tradition of Robert Browning's dramatic monologues, although without the latter's depth psychology. The persona states that he prefers his life as a herdsman to that of the farmer or the soldier. He knows and loves his work. He understands and is proud of his ability:

> O strong men with your best
> I would strive heart to heart;
> I could quiet your herds
> With my words, with my words!

The peasant drover is a hero of daily life. He labors, he struggles, he endures. Like the plougher, he is a part of the land he works. "A Drover" rings with truth. The reader is struck with the familiarity and confidence of a young poet who knows well those who work on the soil.

New Songs also contains Colum's short lyric poems, "The Bells," and "Dream and Shadow." The later is a beautiful love poem to a lovely girl with golden hair:

> Your face has not the bloom I gave
> My dream of you, my dream of you!
> Your eyes have not her eyes' deep hue,
> Nor has your hair the gold I wrought
> Out of my dreams for head of her—
> M Bhron! I thought that dream sheen caught
> From hair of you, from hair of you!
> Pale lips, pale hair, 'tis not your fault:
> A shadow of a dream are you!

"Dream and Shadow" shows Colum at his youthful best, writing songlike, romantic poetry, delicate work with enduring quantity. With the publication of *New Songs* the reading public of Dublin awaited a whole volume of poems from the virile new writer.

Wild Earth (1907)

Colum dedicated his first volume of poetry "to AE who fostered me," and he included "The Plougher," "A Drover," and "A Poor Scholar of the 'Forties" in the collection of twenty-five poems which permanently established his reputation as a major Irish poet and the most important literary spokesman for the Catholic peasant tradition. Furthermore, Colum was recognized as the representative poet of the Irish Midlands.[9]

Wild Earth is the basis of Colum's canon. Although he continued to revise his poetry throughout his life, he seldom deviated from or improved on the clarity, the strength, the Romanticism, the enthusiasm, the vigor, and the lyric quality of these early pieces. Perhaps most important is that the Ireland Colum wrote about while he still lived there and when he was close to both the land and childhood, was an island inhabited by strong, primal people who had little hope or chance to improve the material aspects of their lives and who recognized, in a tragic sense, their own hopelessness. Yet they were a people who endured because of their deep roots in their soil and their ancient traditions, and they persevered because of their courage and their faith. "It is because Colum has lived close to the wild earth of

his native land, tinged as it is with the memory of Rome, that he is
able to achieve these effects. . . ."[10] When Colum left Ireland, his
brave, stark vision of the Irish people slowly faded.

A great strength of *Wild Earth*, perhaps its most enduring quality,
is that the collection is not merely about ploughers and drovers, and
poor old women on the road, but it is primarily about the elemental
nobility of those who live in the ancient ways, close to the soil: it is
about the inherent courage of those who must and do understand life
and death. The characters in its poems are their own symbols. Their
songs are the sole substance of Colum's art.

"The Young Girl" stands for all those maidens who wish to marry,
but alas, inhabit a poor country where men must marry late and
women wear out early. Sadly and vainly she waits for someone to
come and ask for her.

> Oh, if you ask not for me,
> But leave me here instead,
> The narrow, narrow coffin
> Will shortly be my bed.

"Dermott Donn MacMorna," a fine dramatic monologue, is influenced by Synge's play, *The Shadow of the Glen* (1903); both concern
the marriage of a young woman and an older man, a marriage without children. Colum's poem is totally serious, however, while Synge's
play has comic elements. It is a painful, incompatible, frustrating,
arranged relationship. The frustrated wife will leave her husband's
bed and toss over the conventional life to go on the road with her
lover, Dermott, realizing, however, that "the winds do bitter blow."

Colum felt deeply for the plight of women, especially those who
were homeless. In *Wild Earth* there is "An Old Woman of the
Roads," about a woman hoping for sustenance, but accepting the sad
fate decreed for her. She longs for a warm fire and a few pieces of
china to cherish in a little house of her own where she may rest her
weary bones. But she is without rancor, hatred, or a burning sense of
injustice. She only accepts and hopes.

> And I am praying to God on high,
> And I am praying Him night and day,
> For a little house—a house of my own—
> Out of the wind's and rain's way.

The last poem in the 1907 *Wild Earth* is "A Ballad Maker." It tells the tale of a musician who is sorry that he has lost his love, but happy that the experience of losing her has inspired the very ballad he is singing.

> And I who have lost her—the dear, the rare—
> Well, I got me this ballad to sing at the fair,
> 'Twill bring enough money to drown my care,
>   Over the hills and far away.

Thus Colum indicates that the final consolation for the artist is his art itself. Experience, even sad experience, can be turned into song, and song can be turned into solace through drink. The refrain "Over the hills and far away," is nostalgic and sad, but it adds the timelessness of the folk song to the ballad.

In evidencing love of his people and their places by controlling sentimentality, by using sparse but strong language, and by adhering to a regimen of realism, Colum made *Wild Earth* "his most lasting contribution to Irish literature."[11] The poems of *Wild Earth* are now a part of the oral Irish folk tradition.

Studies (1907)

Colum published his verse play *The Miracle of the Corn* along with two short stories, "Eilis: A Woman's Story" and "The Flute-Player's Story" almost simultaneously with *Wild Earth*. He considered *The Miracle of the Corn* as a part of his dramatic canon at this time; thus he did not include the poetic drama with *Wild Earth* and, instead, placed it with the two stories. However, when Colum published *Poems* in 1932 he included *The Miracle of the Corn* in the book's first section "Reminiscence, dramatic Legends, Dramatic Idylls." (We discussed this verse play as drama in chapter two.) As a dramatic poem *The Miracle of the Corn* works a little better than as a play. The reader is able, by slowing down, to enjoy the simple loveliness of the verse. The farmer husband says:

> As air comes from it all—a smell of growing
> Green, growing corn; and I mind that I
> Brought Sheila from her mother's to this house
> Across a field of corn that smelled sweet, sweet,
> and whispered lovingly.

> I cried "O, stir no more!
>   (My breast was touched of tears).
> O pigeons make no stir
>   A childless woman hears."

In "Seed" Colum extols the strength and the glory of regeneration:

> Give me to the Earth.
> With the seed I would enter.
> O! the growth thro' the silence
> From strength to new strength;
> Then the strong bursting forth
> Against primal forces,
> To laugh in the sunshine,
> To gladden the world.

"Seed," later called "The Furrow and the Hearth," evidences Colum's youthful exuberance for life. The poem is affirmative. It exudes energy in both meaning and form.

"A Connachtman" is a nine-stanza ballad filled with humor and pathos. An old peasant singer envisions his own wake. There

> The old men will have their stories
>   Of all the deeds in my days,
> And the young men will stand by the coffin
>   And be sure and clear in my praise.

He sees his death as having mythic qualities as if he were a hero of ancient Ireland:

> And then, between daybreak and dark,
>   And between the hill and the sea,
> Three Women come down from the Mountain
>   Will raise the Keen over me.

Finally, though, the reality and finality of death sinks in. In sadness he exclaims:

> But 'tis my grief that I will not hear,
>   When the cuckoo cries in Glenart,
> That the wind that lifts when the sails are
>   loosed
>   Will never lift my heart.

A different vagrant woman is "The Suilier," later called "What the
Shuiler Said as She Lay by the Fire in the Farmer's House," who expects rewards for her hard life: a house, a servant, leisure to lie in
bed, and "good red gold/to huggle between my breast and my
hands." Colum does not judge her avariciousness. She just is. She is
another part of the great tableau of humanity. Colum is not a critic
of life; he is a chronicler.

The young Colum, of marriage age himself, asks "The Good Men
of Eirinn":

> Are they not the good men of Eirinn
>   Who give not their thought nor their voice
> To fortune, but take without dowry
>   The maids of their choice?

Colum understands, and gently portrays the shock, wonderment,
and pleasure of a young girl's first encounter with the power of sex:

Across the Door

> The fiddles were playing and playing,
>   The couples were out on the floor;
> From converse and dancing he drew me,
>   And across the door.
>
> Ah! strange were the dim, wide meadows,
>   And strange was the cloud-strewn sky,
> And strange in the meadows the corncrakes,
>   And they making cry!
>
> The hawthorn bloom was by us.
>   Around us the breath of the south.
> White hawthorn, strange in the night-time—
>   His kiss on my mouth!

In "No Child" a woman without child is the subject of a beautiful
and delicate lament. The juxtaposition of the sound of pigeons on the
night air with the envisioned touch of a child is most fortunate.

> I heard in the night the pigeons
>   Stirring within their nest:
> The wild pigeons' stir was tender
>   Like a child's hand at the breast.

his native land, tinged as it is with the memory of Rome, that he is able to achieve these effects. . . ."[10] When Colum left Ireland, his brave, stark vision of the Irish people slowly faded.

A great strength of *Wild Earth,* perhaps its most enduring quality, is that the collection is not merely about ploughers and drovers, and poor old women on the road, but it is primarily about the elemental nobility of those who live in the ancient ways, close to the soil: it is about the inherent courage of those who must and do understand life and death. The characters in its poems are their own symbols. Their songs are the sole substance of Colum's art.

"The Young Girl" stands for all those maidens who wish to marry, but alas, inhabit a poor country where men must marry late and women wear out early. Sadly and vainly she waits for someone to come and ask for her.

> Oh, if you ask not for me,
> But leave me here instead,
> The narrow, narrow coffin
> Will shortly be my bed.

"Dermott Donn MacMorna," a fine dramatic monologue, is influenced by Synge's play, *The Shadow of the Glen* (1903); both concern the marriage of a young woman and an older man, a marriage without children. Colum's poem is totally serious, however, while Synge's play has comic elements. It is a painful, incompatible, frustrating, arranged relationship. The frustrated wife will leave her husband's bed and toss over the conventional life to go on the road with her lover, Dermott, realizing, however, that "the winds do bitter blow."

Colum felt deeply for the plight of women, especially those who were homeless. In *Wild Earth* there is "An Old Woman of the Roads," about a woman hoping for sustenance, but accepting the sad fate decreed for her. She longs for a warm fire and a few pieces of china to cherish in a little house of her own where she may rest her weary bones. But she is without rancor, hatred, or a burning sense of injustice. She only accepts and hopes.

> And I am praying to God on high,
> And I am praying Him night and day,
> For a little house—a house of my own—
> Out of the wind's and rain's way.

The long poem's allegorical elements, so blunt upon the stage, and the obviousness of the plot and denouement which a theater audience would find tedious, are simply acceptable structural elements to the reader.

In 1914 Colum left Ireland for America. Slowly he lost touch with Irish psyche as well as Irish soil. His work would undergo a subtle but progressive change based on the distancing of time and place. Much of his poetic energy would go into remaking what he had already accomplished. That accomplishment was best summed up by Ernest Boyd when he wrote that Colum "brought once more the peasant mind into Anglo-Irish poetry, which is thus renewed at the stream from which our national traditions have sprung, for it is the country people who still preserve the Gaelic element in Irish life, the beliefs, the legends and the usages which give us a national identity."[12]

Chapter Four

The Irish-American Poet: 1914–1960

For most of the middle years of Padraic Colum's professional life as a poet, his poetry shows little evidence of creative development or growth. It was as if the maturing and graying man, a part of the New York and international literary scene, was orbiting in the comfortable image of "Irish Poet," rather than accepting and adjusting to his new life as a writer in America and the new realities of a changing and independent Ireland. He was, after all, earning his livelihood largely as a writer of children's books. The exception to this uncomfortable truth was his work on Hawaiian folklore, which will be discussed in chapter 7. In Colum's old age, however, his poetry would bloom again in a vigorous creative renaissance.

The creative slowdown of Colum's middle period is perhaps best represented by his many revisions and reissues of *Wild Earth*. Besides the original Dublin 1907 edition and the 1909 reissue, he brought out a version in America in 1916, and there were international revised editions in 1922, 1927, and 1950. Additionally, the original collection was reworked in the collected editions of 1932 and 1953, and in *The Poet's Circuits: Collected Poems of Ireland* (1960). However, it must be said that the critics never minded the revision and reissues for they always greeted a "new" collection of Colum's verse favorably.

Wild Earth and Other Poems (1916)

Two years after coming to America Colum brought out an expanded version of *Wild Earth* with forty-two poems. It includes "Arab songs," reflecting a long-term interest in what Colum saw as the manly, independent ways of the desert dweller; some translations from the Irish, a lament for bygone days of glory; and the first of his creature poems, "River Mates," which would be retitled "Otters" to fit in with later formats.

"River Mates," a successful piece, seems to have inspired Colum, a lover of animals, to write more poems about beasts. This poem, like many of the later poems, anthropomorphizes the animals, and the tone sounds more like a Viking speaking than a small, water creature, but the poem is strong and it is fun to read and envision. A child, hearing the poem, can appreciate it as much as an adult reading it silently:

River Mates

I'll be an otter, and I'll let you swim
A mate beside me; we will venture down
A deep, full river when the sky above
Is shut of the sun; spoilers are we:—
Thick-coated: no dog's tooth can bite at our veins—
With ears and eyes of poachers: deep-earthed ones
Turned hunters; let him strike past,—
The little vole; my teeth are on an edge
For the King-Fish of the River!

"She Moved Through the Fair," one of the first of Colum's poems to be set to music, is a charming ballad of a young man who loses his love. It has a haunting, extended, literal image, the kind Colum did best. The sad youth remembers how:

She stepped away from me and she moved through the fair,
And fondly I watched her go here and go there. . . .

"Three Spinning Songs" presents three singers: A young girl, an "elder" girl, and an old woman. "Carricknabauna" is the title of the old woman's poignant song in which she calls out to

an oul' trooper . . . riding by
On the road to Carricknabauna

Shamelessly, she offers herself to the handsome, young cavalryman:

I'd spread my cloak for you, young lad,
Were it only the breadth of a farthen. . . .

She wants him to

> Carry me up to the top of the hill
> And show me Carricknabauna!

The old "crone" is begging for the ride up the hill because it was there that the most momentous event of her life took place. It is where she lost her virginity:

> I lost a horse at Cruckmoylinn—
> At the Cross of Brunratty I dropped a limb—
> But I left my youth on the Crown of the hill
> Over by Carricknabauna!

The direction and the sparseness of the poem save it from sentimentality. As with the best of Colum's Irish verse much of the achievement is in what is left unsaid. Colum deftly circumscribes human experience and it is enough.

"The Baltimore Exile," one of the group called "Polonius and the Ballad Singers," is a song of Ireland sung from another land. It could be Colum himself asking:

> The House I was bred in—ah, does it remain?
> Low walls and loose thatch standing lone in the rain,
> With the clay of the walls coming through with its stain,
> Like the blackbird's left nest in the briar!

The "exile" calls from afar for revolt:

> O youth of my Land! Then will no Bolivar
> Ever muster your ranks for delivering war?

Finally, the "exile," who feels he cannot return like a bird to his native land because he is "a bird too old to uncage now," is solaced by art:

> A song is more lasting than the voice of the birds!
> A word is more lasting than the riches of the world!

"I Shall Not Die for Thee" is a love ballad from the Irish about a man desperately trying to survive a love for a beautiful woman who has broken many hearts and is threatening to break his too:

> O Woman, shapely as a swan,
> On your account I shall not die:
> The men you've slain—a trivial clan—
> Were less than I.
>
> I ask shall I die for these—
> For blossom-teeth and scarlet lips?
> And shall that delicate swan shape
> Bring me eclipse?
>
> Well-shaped the breasts and smooth the skin,
> The cheeks are fair, the tresses free—
> And yet I shall not suffer death—
> God over me!
>
> Those even brows, that hair like gold,
> Those languorous tones, that virgin way—
> The flowing limbs, the rounded heel
> Slight men betray!

The beautiful woman has defeated men through her sex appeal and the granting of sexual favors, but the poem's persona feels up to the challenge. He comes from a clever, tough race of men and thus he believes he will persevere and triumph in this skirmish of the war between the sexes:

> O woman, shapely as the swan,
> In a cunning house hard-reared was I:
> O bosom white, O well-shaped palm,
> I shall not die!

This poem is a good example of how Colum's best lyric poetry, in its simple grace and beauty, frustrates literary critics. As L. A. G. Strong says: "The work of Padraic Colum has had little critical attention, not through neglect or ignorance, but because its central quality is one with which literary criticism has little to do. Simplicity cannot be analyzed."[1]

"Old Men Complaining" is like a little dramatic scene in which three old men grouse over the past, their relatives, and their fate. The reader dislikes their complaining and their cantankerousness and he responds to them as prototypes. The poet enters the poem in the last stanza and speaks for all of us:

> I heard them speak—
> The old men heavy on the sod,
> Letting their angers come
> Between them and the thought of God!

Three poems in the 1916 *Wild Earth* are grouped together as "Arab Songs." Of these, "The Parrot and the Falcon" discusses the role of the poet, his temptations and rewards. The Afghan poet is tempted by the promise of fame, offered if he is willing to produce large numbers of familiar-sounding poems:

> "Men come to me;" one says,
> "We have given your verses praise,
> And we will keep your name abreast of the newer names;
> But you must make what accords
> With poems that are household words—
> Your own: write familiar things; to your hundred
> add a score."

However, the Afghan poet, voicing Colum's declaration of artistic independence, his decision to go his own way and avoid the "schools" of his time, says:

> "I have sworn my friends shall have no parrot-speech
> for [from] me.
> Who reads the verse I write
> Shall know the falcon's flight,
> The vision single and sure, the conquest of air and sun!

Thus Colum states that he will continue to write clear, truthful, realistic poems. His poetry will continue to be about the world as it appears. What he observes, he will sing of.

The last poem in the 1916 edition is "For Morfydd." It is a monologue, six stanzas long, in which a young Irishman tells his love of

his dreams of ancient times where he could have been a bowman and
she the daughter of the king. In that Bronze Age of his dreams he
would give his love great gifts.

In the last line of the book, a line with an autobiographical ring,
the young man offers the best gift: "I give what I made, and found,
and caught—a score of songs!"

The poem would be reworked and cannibalized by Colum later: It
became a part of "Reminiscence" in *Dramatic Legends and Other Poems,
Poems,* and *Collected Poems;* and a part of "The Dún" in *The Poet's
Circuits.*

The 1916 edition of *Wild Earth* added several new Irish poems to
Colum's canon, enlarging that body of work which may be his best.
He also begins his "creatures" pieces and he expands the dramatic
monologue as if in preparation for *Dramatic Legends.* Poems like "Interior," in which an old woman dreams of the past and "For Morfydd," however, show Colum already beginning to wax nostalgic
about "Ancient Ireland." Already the reality he wanted to sing of was
becoming somewhat remote for the exile in America.

Dramatic Legends (1922)

Between the publication of the 1916 *Wild Earth* and *Dramatic Legends* in 1922 Colum established a permanent reputation in American
letters through his publication in such prestigious periodicals as *Poetry* (Chicago), the *New Republic;* the *Nation,* the *Dial,* the *North
American Review,* and the *Yale Review.*

Colum dedicates *Dramatic Legends* to his wife with a poem on the
deep source of creativity. At the end of the piece he lovingly says:

> Sweetheart and comrade, I gave you
> The waters' marches and the forest's bound,
> The valley-filling cloud, the trees that set
> The rains beneath their roots, out of this well.

The world the poet creates, as expressed in the following poems, is
given as an offering to love and companionship.

Dramatic Legends begins with sixteen short poems in a section
called "Poems: Country Songs." Colum is trying to maintain the

Irish connection but is not succeeding. The lyrics are forced; the language has turned literary as in "Men on Islands":

> Can it be that never more
> Men will grow on Islands?
> Ithaka and Eriskey,
> Iceland and Tahiti!
> ....
> Crete and Corsica, Mitylene,
> Aran and Iona!

Here, of course, Colum is trying to establish a literary connection between the heroic age of Ireland and the heroic ages of other cultures, but the poem is certainly no peasant "country song."

In "Lament" Colum's artful simplicity has turned to prosaic denotation:

> Now the child who gathered the nuts,
> And brought them to me through the wood—
> The child who gathered the nuts,
> That day, from our life is gone.

In "Legend" Colum sings of the importance of traditional song, learned from the old, in the creation of a nation's destiny and a human being's fate.

He includes an elegy to the martyred Roger Casement in "Poems: Country Songs"along with a memorial piece entitled "The Rune-Master," for the German translator of Irish legends, Kuno Meyer.

The poem in "Poems: Country Songs" that most recalls the power evidenced in *Wild Earth* is "The Poor Girl's Meditation." The poem quickly establishes a dramatic situation. A poor peasant servant girl is sitting at night by a fire. She prays that her lot will improve both in respect to material wealth and to love:

> May I never leave this world
> Until my ill-luck is gone;
> Till I have cows and sheep
> And the lad that I love for my own:
> I would not think it long,
> The night I would lie at his breast,
> And the daughters of spite, after that,
> Might say the thing they liked best.

But she knows that she has little chance to win the man she wants:

> When I bethought on the lad
> That I left on the brow of the hill,
> I wept from dark until dark,
> And my cheeks have the tear-tracks still.

Finally, in despair, she calls for the minimum respect, consideration for her unfortunate lot:

> And, O, young lad that I love,
> I am no mark for your scorn:
> All you can say of me
> Is undowered I was born.

The pathos of "The Poor Girl's Meditation" is genuine. The poem has all the ring of the anonymous folk song, the effect Colum continued to strive for but seldom achieved after 1916. However, the poem, as Colum acknowledged, is an adaptation of an adaptation. Douglas Hyde, in *Love Songs of Connacht,* had made a literal translation from the Old Irish and then had written a new version of the poem.[2] Colum reworked Hyde's poem successfully.

The second section of *Dramatic Legends* is entitled "Creatures and Things Seen." In it Colum adds seven animal poems to the menagerie he began in the 1916 *Wild Earth,* and he presents a small group of other poems in which, for example, "In the Carolina Woods" and "An Indian Showing Feats," he attempts to come to terms, poetically, with his new country. It does not work. However, the creature poems, soon to be part of a book by that name, are among Colum's best short works of the period.

"For Colum, as for other Irish writers, the worship of freedom [was] in some measure a subliminal wish for Ireland's freedom and independence."[3] "The Wild Ass," the first of the creature poems in "Creatures and Things Seen," is an anthropomorphized animal who has no respect for past imperial power. His hooves spurn "the tombs of Archaemedian kings" and all of fallen "rugged Tartary." The wild ass stands alone, is free, and unafraid:

> The wild horse from the herd is plucked
> To bear a saddle's weight;
> The boar is one keeps covert, and

> The wolf runs with a mate;
> But he's the solitary of space,
> Curbless and unbeguiled;
> The only being that bears a heart
> Not recreant to the wild.

Once more Colum is expressing his patriotism in a subtle and symbolic way. To his credit, the poet is very seldom a chauvinistic flagwaver. Instead, he often implies his hope that humankind may experience the freedom that, as in other creatures, is a basic gift of nature.

Similarly, "Vultures" who are "Angels of Foulness" because they are "fierce against the dead," illustrates Colum's belief that it is evil to enslave body or spirit:

> Foul-feathered and scald-necked,
> They sit in evil state;
> Raw marks upon their breasts
> As on men's wearing chains.

And the poor "pigeons" are harem slaves:

> When we'd less years
> We bartered for, bought you—

"The Bird of Paradise" has all the opulence of John Masefield's "Cargoes." Although written later, it is very much an Edwardian poem with its personification, rich imagery, and near rhymes:

> With sapphire for her crown,
> And with the Libyan wine
> For lustre of her eyes;
> With azure for her feet
> (It is her henna stain);
> Then iris for her vest,
> Rose, ebony, and flame,
> She lives a thing enthralled,
> In forests that are old,
> As old as is the moon.

There are poems to "The Bison" and "The Humming Bird," but the most evocative of the creature poems in *Dramatic Legends* is "The Monkeys." It begins with an eye-catching image:

> Two little creatures
> With faces the size of
> A pair of pennies
> Are clasping each other.

Not only does the reader instantly grasp the size of the tiny faces but she sees the dark copper color too. And then, following immediately is the surge of sympathy for the imprisoned animals:

> "Ah, do not leave me,"
> One says to the other,
> In the high monkey-
> Cage in the beast-shop.

The monkeys, after all, are like little people with shaking hearts and their being lost, their loneliness, and their need for love in a hostile world are shared by us all. However, the poem's success is largely due to the iteration of the penny image as in "the penny-small faces" (the pennies, of course, are old-style Irish or British coppers, not the U.S. cent) and also to the human connection as when in the end the monkeys are seen:

> With faces the size of
> A pair of pennies,
> And voices as low as
> The flow of my blood.

"Reminiscence" is a fourteen-part potpourri of Irish experiences. The verse forms vary. There are lyric poems and dramatic monologues. Colum depicts rural and urban scenes, peasant characters, and dreams of Ireland's heroic past. He borrows from early work, particularly "For Morfydd" in the 1916 *Wild Earth*. The total effect of the section is that of a sentimental memory.

By far the largest section of *Dramatic Legends* is the first section from which the book title is taken. "Dramatic Legends" contains four long pieces two of which are one-act plays, "Swift's Pastoral" and

"The Miracle of the Corn," reprinted from *Studies* and discussed in chapter two. In "Swift's Pastoral" Jonathan Swift tells a story to Esther Vanhomrigh, his friend, as they stroll in St. Patrick's Cathedral, Dublin. The tale is one of a harper's unrequited love. It symbolizes Swift's love for his "Stella" and it is told with humor and pathos. Swift in Ireland walks "Upon a ground that's drenched with tears. . . ." He breathes "An air that's thickened with men's darkened spirits." Jonathan Swift represented a special problem for Colum and many other Irish Catholic writers, the problem of the English or Anglo-Irish Protestant artist in Ireland. It was the essential problem of the Pale and it was unresolvable: how were they to relate to and evaluate the work of earlier Anglo-Irish writers: Swift, Wilde, Shaw—perhaps even Yeats and Lady Gregory, too?

"The Bird of Jesus" is a narrative poem set at the time of Jesus' boyhood. The narrator, a lad of the same age, sees the young Jesus turn clay to a living bird. The poem is a child's parable, much like a Christmas story. It extols the purity and grace of youth.

"The Laments of Queen Gormlai" are renderings of four of the eleven poems attributed to the tenth-century Irish queen and translated into English by several translators. Queen Gormalai laments the death of her husband, King Niall Blackknee, in battle near Dublin at the hands of the Norsemen in 917. The poems sound like Anglo-Saxon poetry with kennings and verse forms more alliterative than is Colum's usual practice.

Dramatic Legends and Other Poems, although it was critically well received, was not a giant step forward for the poet. Instead it seems now to indicate a recession from the intensity and clarity of the Irish vision of Colum's earlier poetry. Perhaps realizing that the creature poems in the collection were the most promising, he went on to pursue his growing bestiary.

Creatures (1927)

Creatures contains eighteen new poems and ten poems previously published in the 1916 *Wild Earth* or *Dramatic Legends:* "David Ap Gwillam at the Mass of the Birds," "Otters," "Pigeons," "Wild Ass," "Monkeys," "Bison," "Bird of Paradise," "Humming Bird," "Vultures," and "Hornets," a revision of "The Hornet's Nest" in *Dramatic Legends.* The volume is finely illustrated by Boris Artzybasheff. Perhaps because of the Irish Civil War, Colum seems temporarily to have lost interest in writing poetry about people. Life in New York City may have distracted him from the Irish peasant and land. Most probable of all, *Creatures* afforded the author an opportunity to explore his love for color, shape, movement, and living things.

It is perhaps both important and interesting to note that Colum's animals, those listed above and the others in *Creatures*, are, for the most part, like his people, the lowly ones. He does not write poems to lions, tigers, or bears. "Jackdaw" presents a world where dogs are "rubbing for fleas," and those birds, like vagrants, scavenge for rags. One

> Held a bright rag up
> Like a banner won,
> And went and hid it
> Behind a stone!

The small and humble creatures of the world have their small, humble victories.

Colum's "Crows" are as common as people. They are "The first live things we see in the mornings." But at night they move, like vagabonds, unseen

> Except by eyes that are like to their own
> Trespassers' eyes!

The "Plovers" are "wandering and impetuous." Colum, the exile, the traveler to America, France, and Hawaii, identifies with the vagabond birds:

> My thoughts are like the Plovers' flight,
> Unguided, nestless, without bourn,
> Wandering and impetuous,
> Turning and flying to return.

In "Asses" lowly animals and their peasant owners are again the heroes of Colum's world. The poem is set at a country fair where the proud, prancing horses shame the beasts of burden. The owners of the fine horses refuse gold for their pets. They are the human equivalent to the vain beasts, but there is a peasant woman who has come to the fair in a cart and who has two asses. Colum sees her as a queen

"On the deck of her ship." The woman and her work animals, naturally, "like the flowers in the grasses," are the finest of the living.

The "Swallow," surely the most common of birds, has his wings likened to scimitars and his eyes to those of a genie, as Colum exercises both his love for the exotic East and his love for the little ordinary bits of life. A major technique of Colum's is to point out the beauty, the variegation, and the unusual in what on the literal level seems so ordinary—like a swallow.

The "Crane" is called upon, like a metal detector, to find things such as

> The pennies that were laid upon the eyes
> Of old, wise men I knew.

A "Singing Bird," now captive, remembers the forest songs of freedom. "The Little Fox" is also a slave pet, walked like a dog on a leash, and lost in civilization:

> He goes upon the sidewalk; houses tower;
> Men trample; horses rear; he drags his leash.

Even in "Aquarium Fish" the "Most rootless of all beings" is trapped, like the humans who watch it. Fish and humankind ask: "Who closed/up the depth to us?" The "Snake" is also a creature made by "The Wise Elohim." Its temptation is mercy and identification with humanity. The "bare and voiceless" beast is also a part of God's plan and deserving of consideration and respect.

"Night Flyers," "Macaws," and "Condors," join "The Resplendent Quetzal-bird" in Colum's green and glorious aviary, where the Guatemalan bird has "sunken all colours/Into glory of greenness!" The macaw has "green wings and yellow breasts." The bird is like "A green sun shining on a sea of yellow." In fact, Colum enjoys the sight of the colorful birds so much that he humbly states: "Their greens and yellows are better than a song. . . ."

Three hunting scenes, reflecting Colum's abiding interest in ancient civilizations, in this instance the Minoan, the Celtic, and the Indian, round out *Creatures* along with a poem on "Sandalwood." The hunting scenes at first seem incongruous in a book exalting animals, but the poems treat the game with reverence and dignity, and they serve to show the traditional interrelationship between ancient heroic man and the hunted animal, a relationship which required courage and respect on the part of the hunter with a bow or spear.

Creatures is a satisfying collection of poetry. Its goals are limited. It sets out to present, and succeeds in presenting, a bestiary of great beauty, like an Irish monk's book of the Middle Ages. Finally, although limited in profundity and deep insight into the human condition, *Creatures* is a delightful celebration of life.

Old Pastures (1930)

Old Pastures contains thirty new poems, including five short pieces collected under the title of "Hawaii" which are free translations from the native literature. Other renderings or translations in the collection include "At the Fore of the Year" from a traditional Irish song, "A Man Bereaved" from Scottish Gaelic, and another poem about "Queen Gormlai" from medieval Irish.[4] As with *Dramatic Legends,* many of the poems were first offered in prestigious American periodicals such as the *Dial,* the *Commonweal,* the *New Republic,* the *Saturday Review of Literature, Scribner's Magazine,* and *Harper's Bazaar.* The only Irish periodical acknowledged in *Old Pastures* is the *Irish Statesman.*[5] The Irish poet, Padraic Colum, is in fact doing most of his publication, poems and collections, with American publishers. *Old Pastures* adds little that is memorable to the Colum canon. The poet was losing, at least for the time being, identification with turn-of-the-century Irish peasantry, and he was not comfortable in the temporary role of international poet writing on such diverse cultures as the Hawaiian, American, and Western European.

The initial poem in *Old Pastures,* "Dublin Roads," continues the iterative road motif in Colum's poetry and prose. The fourteen five-line stanzas present a young boy's views of the exotic happenings on the road, seeing the carts, animals, and human bearers. Peacocks, pigeons, robins, and other birds sing and cry along the way. It is a wonderful world. The boy persona and the middle-aged poet both would like to "go back along the road."

Four poems about plant life follow "Dublin Roads": "Fuchsia Hedges in Connacht," "Woodbine," "Lilac Blossoms," and "Briar Blossoms." The first piece is typical of Colum's poems of religious experiences in which he expresses religiosity by the recognition and realization of historical roots and the identification of religious anal-

ogy in nature, rather than by an epiphany. The Irish countryside itself confirms his Catholicism. The hedges exist because

> . . . some saint of Eirinn wandering far
> Found you and brought you here—

Originally the fuchsia hedges, the poet thinks,

> . . . came from some old Roman land—
> Most alien, but most Catholic are you:
> Your purple is the purple that enfolds,
> In Passion Week, the Shrine,
> Your scarlet is the scarlet of the Wounds. . . .

Thus the beautiful plant is symbolic of the Church itself. The hedge,
like Roman Catholicism, comes from an alien land, and its flowering
is like the colorful glory of the places and the garb of its ancient religion. Colum's devotion is the kind that is the deepest, the surest,
and the most unquestioning.

In "Woodbine" he praises its scent which can give delight to an
old man and which is a seductive perfume for a young girl on her
way to a dance. The ephemeralness of "Lilac Blossoms" reminds its
reader of his own brief mortality:

> We, we are gone without a word that praised us—
> You did not know how short the playing-time!

The "Briar Blossoms," in contrast to the woodbine and the lilac, are
scentless and, like the meek and humble of the earth, live "Beside
down-tumbled Barns. . . ."

Poems about men and women in *Old Pastures* include "At the Fore
of the Year," "A Man Bereaved," "Branding the Foals," and "Scanderbeg." They are the most moving and intense pieces in the collection. The first mentioned is a metrically tight, but unrhymed ballad
in which a young man has fallen in love with a girl he saw in church
on Candlemass Day, and whom he has courted with "bragging and
lies," hoping then to "win her with praises." But he has not been
doing so well. In fact, he has not done well at all. Instead:

> . . . through Spring and through Summer she has left me
>   to rise
> Every day with a pain that will slay me!

The poem is gently ironic. The plotting boy is hoist on his own pe-
tard and the girl, whom he tried to seduce, has coolly won mastery
over him.

"A Man Bereaved" is a strong dramatic monologue. A peasant
farmer's young wife has died and he grieves for her. He misses hearing her sing and seeing her "plaiting her long locks." The lament is
somewhat marred, however, because he seems to miss his deceased
wife's manual service as much as anything else.

"Branding the Foals" is perhaps Colum's most sexually passionate
poem. A man seeing the woman he burningly desires approach "car-
rying the lighted coals/and branding tool" states:

> What need have I for what is in her hands,
> If I lay hand upon a hide it brands,
> And grass, and trees, and shadows, all are fire!

The man feels that he is on fire himself. The forthrightness and sex-
uality of "Branding the Foals" is quite unusual for Colum.

"Scanderbeg," with its startling imagery, may be the most provocative and satisfying poem in *Old Pastures*. A man and a woman are
visiting a tombstone memorial to a learned knight, descended from
Scanderbeg, a conquerer of the Turks and savior of Europe. The man
is full of history and reverence as

> Two hundred years' battling in Europe at the name of
>   Scanderbeg
> Spun through my mind as a curlew cried overhead!

But, alas, as for the woman:

> She sat on the wall and dangled her silk-stockinged legs,
> Saying, "I'll not have them all stung for any old man
>   who is dead."

The persona dreams of battles. The practical girl does not want to
risk the nettles. Her irreverence, indifference, and practicality hu-
manizes her even as they proclaim her ignorance. Colum implies here
and elsewhere that men are the idealists and dreamers, while women
are more often the practical half of the human race.

The Irish history and mythology poems in *Old Pastures* are "Queen
Gormlai," "Breffne Caoine," "At Cashel," and "Brendan." Colum

blends history, myth, and invention skillfully, especially in regard to the sailor-monk Brendan. "Much of the charm of Colum's poetry and children's stories lies in the tantalizing ring of truth in his legends and in the unexpected apocryphal in what seems to be realistic."[6]

In "The Landing" Colum writes of returning to Ireland by sea as he had several times. His lost island home is still dear to his heart sixteen years after leaving.

In "Song of Starlings" too there is an exile's lament:

> . . . we hear the starlings
> As we have heard them often in other cities,
> Around other cupolas, along other cornices,
> In sunless parks bunched on the tops of trees,
> And see around us bleak, monotonous fields
> Our hearts must ever hold—theirs are these songs—
> These are the songs that most touch us exiles!

"The Condors in the Jardin des Plantes" and "The Bat" are two new creature poems. The condors in the cage are also weary prisoners of their "shuttered, iron-heavy wings," "ironically" the instruments of freedom through flight. The bat in Colum's poem is lost in daylight, out of his element, the night. Both poems are in essence about alienation and loss of freedom.

"Blades" and "Odysseus" are political poems. The former, subtle but oddly militant for Colum, is a poem about an itinerant knife-grinder who comes to the village and, as he sharpens a variety of knives realistically described by Colum, chastises the men for their inability to act fiercely against their oppressors and their enemy. He leaves the village without a blessing after sharpening knives for three young men. The poem ends with a vivid and shocking irony:

> And three who brought back sharpened blades
> To their fathers' stalls by the Tan-yard Side,
> And then stayed while a blackbird cried
> Quietly by their groundsills—
> The butcher's daughter,
> The cobbler's daughter,
> The hawker's daughter,
> Were lost on the hills!

"Odysseus" is an *In Memoriam* for Colum's old friend, Arthur Griffith, Ireland's first president. The poet, who had begun a biography of Griffith, saw him as an adventurer, like the Greek hero, who ". . . made/The plan that drove the wasters from the house. . . ." Colum's affection and admiration for the journalist who had helped him so much in his youth was very great. The poet well paid his debt of gratitude in poetry and prose.

The remainder of *Old Pastures* contains incidental and occasional pieces, and the five Hawaiian poems. The latter fail to evoke a sense of the culture, and the occasional interjection of a Hawaiian phrase seems unconvincing and gratuitous. *Old Pastures* evidences a slight tiring in the poet, a draining of vitality, a lack of direction. It is as if his art were slowly drying up in a soil only superficially hospitable to the Irish cutting.

Poems (1932)

In *Poems* Colum collected and republished the verse that had appeared in *New Songs, Wild Earth,* the 1916 *Wild Earth, Dramatic Legends, Creatures,* and *Old Pastures.* The poet reordered much of his work as he would do again in *The Poet's Circuits* (1960). *Poems* has five sections: "Reminiscence, Dramatic Legends, Dramatic Idylls"; "Wild Earth"; "Other Lands and Seas"; "Creatures"; and "Old Pastures." Examples of change from the original collections and groupings are: "An Idyll" and "The Wayfarer" in the 1916 *Wild Earth* are now in "Other Lands and Seas"; "In the Carolina Woods" in *Dramatic Legends* is also in "Other Lands and Seas" as is "First East to West Atlantic Flyers" and "Hawaii" from *Old Pastures.* "Hunting Scenes from the Minoan," "Hunting Scene from the Indian," and "Hunting Scenes from the Hawaiian" from *Creatures* are placed in "Reminiscence, Dramatic Legends, and Dramatic Idylls" as is "The Burial of St. Brendan" which was "Brendan" in *Old Pastures.*

Poems indicates that before the age of fifty Colum had written pretty much all of the memorable lyric poetry of his lifetime. From 1932 on the poet would get much mileage from reading, reordering, and republishing his earlier work. Still his collection in *Poems* is no mean achievement. *Poems* is a valuable contribution to English-language poetry of the twentieth century.

There are seven poems in *Poems* not previously collected: "The Knitters," "Folding Hour," and "A Saint" in "Wild Earth"; and "Laburnums," "Verses for Alfeo Faggi's Stations of the Cross," "The Old College of the Irish, Paris," and "Ave Atque Vale" in "Old Pastures." "The Knitters" is reminiscent of "Spinning Songs," which

Colum placed just before in *Poems*. However, it is about the cottage
women, not by them. The poor women have

> . . . come to own
> That all the works we do
> Repeat a wonted toil.

The poet's only prayer for "these knitters at their doors" is that they
can learn, in the absence of beloved freedom, to do their repetitive
work "with grace and in content." The village men and even the animals, alas, are freer than the women, for the "men are tramping
home" "while goats bleat from the hills." "The Knitters," although
quite a minor piece, fits in with Colum's Irish peasant poetry.

In "A Saint" Colum again alludes to the absence of freedom that
poverty means for women. A parade in honor of a saint finds

> The stir of children with fresh dresses on,
> And men who meet and say unguarded words,
> And women from the coops
> Of drudgeries released.

"Folding Hour" follows "The Knitters" in *Poems*. It is a poem about
night and a boy cowherd who peacefully sings to his cattle: "Night's
a good herd . . . she brings all things back."

"Laburnums" fits in well with "Lilac Blossoms" and "Fuchsia
Hedges in Connacht" which follow it. The poem opens with a startling image:

> Over old walls the Laburnums
> hang cones of fire.

The flowers of the tree cover the ugly parts of a country which has
"no lindens, no palms, no cedars of Lebanon." The poet uses the
"cone fire" image other times, and the refrain burns out the sight of
the "mould, old men and old maids." Finally, a glory comes to the
impoverished Irish town:

> The bare and dusty streets have now the Laburnums,
> Have now cones of fire!

"Verses for Alfeo Faggi's Stations of the Cross" describes the sculptured bronze fourteen stations in Chicago's St. Thomas's Church. It is one of Colum's most religious poems, with little in the way of didacticism. Each short stanza records the poet's deep-felt pity as well as describes the scene.

"The old College of the Irish, Paris" is a pedestrian, historical description. "Ave Atque Vale" is a traditional farewell, this at a brother's grave to which the persona has traveled from beyond the seas. Of the new pieces in *Poems* "The Knitters," "Folding Hours," and "Laburnums" fit in with Colum's early Irish peasant poetry and "Verses for Alfeo Faggi's Stations of the Cross" stems from the allegory, "The Bird of Jesus." However, these new poems show no sign of development, experimentation, or growth in Colum's work. He seems to have begun to think almost as much about new ways to present old material as about the creation of fresh and exciting poetry.

The Story of Lowry Maen (1937)

The Story of Lowry Maen is Padraic Colum's longest poem, an epic narrative in seven parts and in over 1800 lines of blank verse. Colum says "The theme of the narrative is the break-up of an ancient order and the coming of a new order. The order that is broken up is that of the Bronze Age in Ireland; the order that takes its place is that of the Iron Age."[7]

Colum "attempts to create a popular Irish epic,"[8] one written in a language clear enough and simple enough that Irish school children could memorize it as perhaps Greek children had once memorized the *Iliad*. He assumes the role of an ancient storyteller stopping, while on his way to compete at a fair, to tell his tale in a nobleman's house. The choice of the end of the Age of Bronze in Ireland for the time reflects Colum's nostalgia for that moment of ancient glory. Early in the poem Croftnie the Harp-player, the Colum persona, prophesies the future to the young prince:

> "The change, I think, that's coming over all.
> Your father's grandfather, Ugony the Great,
> Had set a mould of custom round men's ways:
> He lived so long that he

Had broken Change to be a household beast. . . .
But long-lived Ugony the Great is dead:
Now Change will growl and snarl and tear flesh—
I see her widely opened wild-lynx eyes." (p. 4)

The Story of Lowry Maen's hero is not the harper, however, but the prince, whose first name is like the Irish word *lahaid*, meaning "speaks," and whose last name is Irish for "speechless"; thus his name means "speechless speaks" because, when a boy, he was struck dumb at the horror of his father's murder at the hands of his uncle; but his speech returns when he defeats his uncle's son on a playing field. Lowry Maen is like Colum, an exile. After years of trial, tribulation, and careful planning, he returns to his homeland leading a mighty army and recovers his usurped throne.

Colum's epic of ancient Ireland fails. It is not memorable either in story or language. The poet's gentle, nonbelligerent nature works against him here. The national epic as a type requires emphasis on warrior skills. It thrives on descriptions of battle, hand-to-hand and one-to-one combats; feats of daring and courage; success against great odds; and an implication that divine destiny has selected a larger-than-life hero to shape a national destiny.

The Story of Lowry Maen has little of the above. When Lowry comes to battle with his cousin and defeats him because of his superior iron weapons, the narrator refuses to gratify his listeners with a description of the fray. For Colum's personal idea of courage was never military prowess, even though he often had to write about it, particularly, and ironically, in his prose for children. Courage for him was the long-term, stoic endurance of the peasant willing to wait out the sojourn of the conqueror, even if it would take centuries, or the patience and self-sacrifice of the Christian saint, rooted in morality and belief in reward after death.

Furthermore, Colum seems to have been repelled by the need to portray his characters, particularly his hero, with the necessary semibarbaric fierceness and cruelty, possibly in part because he was hoping for a school audience as well as an adult one. Still, the dramatic effect is lost.

The Story of Lowry Maen's strength is simultaneously its weakness; that is, Colum loves to chronicle the domestic activities of peasants and nobles in their daily lives. The historical detail, the homey description, and the love of the beautiful give the reader pleasure but deflect the epic intent. In essence *The Story of Lowry Maen* fails as a national epic because it is too close to a children's fairy tale. Colum never again attempted to write an epic poem.

Flower Pieces (1938)

Padraic Colum's long sojourn in France in the 1930s gave rise to *Flower Pieces,* a group of seventeen short poems somewhat related to the work of the French Impressionist painters, but published in Dublin in a limited edition of three hundred copies. His love of bright colors and the small beauties of life manifested itself in the writing of these short, delicate poems.

"Hollyhocks" have

> . . . leaves too broad
> For garden flowers,
> And stalks too lofty.

They are like beautiful people with ". . . faces lustered/Pink, white and coral."

"Lilies are part of the Universal Church," "at the White Mass" where

> . . . they are garnished
> As for that miracle
> That turns the natural
> Into supernatural.

"Morning Glories" announce the day:

> Morning with its stillness, and these flowers
> Offering themselves above the trellises. . . .

Not surprisingly, Colum often likens his flowers to women. The "Mimosa" is a "Princess . . . in veils of gold," "The Hydrangea" are "nunnery girls," and "Marigolds" "honour/The name of Mary."

Colum seems to love deeply the various shades of red. The Hibiscus's ". . . scarlet darkens like the stain in dust/Where walked the daughter of Herodias." "Geraniums are the reddest of all homely things." "Poppies" look

> Like red-capped outlaws on Justicar's land,
> Like Moghuls in a square of Samarkand.

And lastly, "Oleander Blossoms" are like "some red-crowned city."

Colum saw his "Roses" in Spain, growing "Out of old walls/In the Alhambra."

Of "Wallflowers" Colum simply says that there are "none so pleasant." Often in Colum's poetry vivid color is a special gift from God, the purpose of which is to serve His greater glory. The "buoyant blossoms" of "Nasturtiums" "redeem/much dinginess." "The Veronicas before Dublin Houses" "have purple plume that the butterflies go to" and "the rain-drops fall from [them] with singular purity."

"Acanthus leaves" are "like Homeric imagery," while "Tulips" bear

> . . . a Persian name,
> Or Turkish one . . .
> Tulips that are receptacles of light.

Colum's flowers take him to the exotic as well as the homey.

Lastly, "Briar Blossoms" is reprinted in *Flower Pieces* from *Old Pastures*. Colum would continue to write flower pieces and would publish an enlarged collection in *The Vegetable Kingdom* (1954).

The Collected Poems of Padraic Colum (1953)

From 1938 to 1953 Colum published no collection of verse. His creative energies were absorbed by his children's books and folklore and in the writing of his second novel *The Flying Swans* (1957), and his biography of Arthur Griffith, *Ourselves Alone* (1959), both to be published when Colum was in his late seventies.

In fact *Collected Poems* is essentially a reprint of *Poems* (1932). Of the 109 pieces in the book, 97 are from *Poems;* "Macaws," from *Creatures,* and somehow left out of *Poems,* now appears in the "Creatures" section of *Collected Poems.* There are only eleven new poems in the book. The fixtures of Colum's poetic canon remained unchanged for the most part from 1932 to the publication of *Vegetable Kingdom* in 1954, when his poetic renaissance began.

In the "Reminiscence, Dramatic Legends" section ("dramatic idylls" is dropped) of *Collected Poems* Colum omitted "Indian" and

"Minoan" while adding "King Cahill's Farewell to the Rye Field" and "Old Song Re-sung." "King Cahill's Farewell to the Rye Field" is a patriotic ballad written to be sung to the traditional Irish melody, "The Londonderry Air."

"An Old Song Re-sung" is a first-person ballad in which an Irish swain, walking through Dublin on a midnight two centuries ago, sees a beautiful Spanish girl, takes her for a coach ride, is intercepted by her underworld lover, Tiger Roache, a kind of Mac-the-Knife, and is mortally wounded in a duel. He dies with a joke on his lips:

> But, O ye bucks of Dublin city,
> If I should see at twelve of the night,
> In any chamber, such lovely lady
> Washing her feet by candle light
> ....
> Your blades be dimmed! I'd whisper her
> And take her for a midnight stroll!

No more coach rides for him! On foot it is safer. One can always forget the blade and run.

This poem is one of Colum's more sensual ones. His exotic women are seldom nice Irish Catholic girls (although occasionally an old woman may remember a youthful fling) but exotic creatures like this:

> . . . Spanish lady
> Washing her feet by candle light.
> First she washed them
> Then she dried them,
> All by a fire of amber coals,
> In all my life I never did see
> A maid so neat about the soles.

"An Old Song Re-sung" presents Colum's sense of humor at its finest. Gently, he makes fun of youthful infatuation and the sexual drive that leads a young man to danger and derring-do.

Colum added two poems to the "Wild Earth" section of *Collected Poems*: "Achill Girl's Song" and "The Charm." The former is a worthy addition, although a translation from the Irish, to Colum's early, peasant poetry. In a delicate four-stanza paragraph, reminiscent of

"The Poor Girl's Meditation," a girl, in love with a boy who as yet
has not come and asked for her hand in marriage, says:

> Oh, if you ask not for me,
> But leave me here instead,
> The petticoat in dye-pot here
> Will never fast its red
>
> For me upon the well-slope
> To wear on Finnian's Day—
> My dress will be the sheet bleached there,
> My place, below the clay!

"The Charm" is founded on the belief, as legend would have it, that
water found by chance in a hollow stone can give the finder strength
and the ability to command, provided he knows the right charm to
speak:

> I dip my fingers and sprinkle,
> While three times over I say,
> "Chance-bound and chance-found water
> Can take a numbness away."

The similarity to dipping fingers into a font of holy water in church
is obvious. Colum, of course, means no "Black Mass" sacrilege.
Rather, he sees nature here as the true church of Irish nationalism,
since this "holy water" may give birth to a needed and valuable
leader:

> . . . on the morrow
> I shall rise with spirit alive;
> Gallant amongst the gallant,
> I shall speak and lead and strive.

Furthermore, by implication the miracle of the water is needed if Ireland is to find champions to lead her back to early Christian, even
pre-Christian greatness.

Colum dropped "To a Poet" and "First East to West Atlantic
Flyers," and he added four poems to the "Other Lands and Seas" sec-
tion of *Collected Poems*: "Kalmuch Bride," "A Seer," "The City
Clocks," and "Young Girl: Annam." In "Kalmuch Bride" again a

girl waits for her man to come to her, and except for words like "scimitar" and "daughter of the Khan" she could just as easily be an Irish peasant colleen. Similarly, the "Young Girl: Annam" waits for a lover by her garden and the only thing Annamese is the mention of bamboo.

"The City Clocks" has a fine image for a refrain:

> The City clocks point out the hours—
> They look like moons on their darkened towers.

"A Seer" predicts the victory of a Red Revolution. The "red songs" will move "White swords" and "white-faced throngs" until "that wild, white thing will lose." The poem, all in quotes, is pusillanimously defensive, as if Colum feared appearing too radical.

In the "Old Pastures" section he added: "The Dead Player: In Memory of Dudley Digges," "In Memory of Thomas Hughes Kelly," and "Before the Fair." The first two would reappear in *Irish Elegies* (1958, 1961, 1966), the Digges poem enlarged. Digges was the actor who played opposite Maude Gonne in the first production of Yeats's *Kathleen ni Houlihan* and was Colum's friend in the Abbey Company. The poem to Kelly is a thank you to the wealthy American who was his benefactor in both Ireland and America:

> And he was raised as with a prime of strength
> That matched the bounty that was his; I knew
> He had been choosen for a task beyond
> Our world's ken, and had accomplished it.

"Before the Fair," the last poem in *Collected Poems,* is a piece in the early tradition of Colum's peasant verse, seemingly more fitting in the "Wild Earth" section along with "She Moved through the Fair." "Before the Fair" is a ballad in which a young man approaches a fair "With thoughts of lust and labour,/And bargain in my heart."

Although *Collected Poems* added very little to Colum's canon, the book was well received critically. Many critics had not read *Poems* and, of course, twenty-one years had passed since the publication of the first collection. There was a whole new generation of critics and readers to charm. The reception of *Collected Poems* set Colum to writing and publishing poetry again with a renewed vigor.

The Vegetable Kingdom (1954)

Padraic Colum was fond of his *Flower Pieces* and sought a larger audience. The University of Indiana Press provided the opportunity. The poet took the seventeen poems from *Flower Pieces,* made a few changes in them, added "Lilac Blossoms" and "Woodbine" from *Old Pastures,* and "Laburnums" from *Poems,* and then filled out his garden of verses with "Sunflower," a "Catalpa Tree," "Olive Trees," a "Poplar Tree," "Ivies," "Dahlias," a "Peach Tree with Fruit," a "Pomegranate Tree with Fruit," a "Trumpet Vine," "Pansies," "Copper Beeches," "Oleander Blossoms," "Spanish Mosses," "Water Lilies," "Flowering Quince," "Tiger Lilies," "Stocks of Pinks or Gillyflowers," and a gardener—or really a gardener's prayer: "To Saint Fiacre, Patron of Gardens."

Column, with delight, renews his friendship and love for the little beauties of creation. His eye for detail and color is as sharp as ever. The poems smile. The "Sunflower" is a falling sun: "Its gold bestrewn and its head downbent," and in a poem from *Flower Pieces* now enlarged:

> The gold, the bronze, the red, the bright-swart Tulips!
> ....
> [are] flowers fit
> To go with vestments red on Pentacost.

A sense of religious and humanitarian service pervades many of the new garden poems as in "Tulips." The "Catalpa Tree" serves

> . . . like men of good heart who proffer all,
> Descending branches held out boons for us.

God through nature shelters and blesses humankind. "Olive Trees" also are given to stewardship "And are of man's domain as oxen are." The "Poplar Tree" is special to Colum for it is a "Child of the Celtic Lands. . . ."

"Irises" stun the poet with their variegated beauty; "argent, purple, azure and pale gold"; they are as the glory of the cathedral window: "colors doubled like two stains in glass."

Like "Acanthus Leaves" in *Flower Pieces,* the "Dahlias" remind Colum of ancient Greece for they are

> Yellow as masks of gold,
> Dark red like wine the Sea-kings pour from galleys.
> And pink as clouds the early oarsman . . . sees.

The "Peach Tree with Fruit" and the "Pomegranate Tree with Fruit" are rich, giving, and sculpted to beauty like woman's, while the "Copper Beech" are "Dark ponderous trees . . . Talmudic in their alienness."

The "Trumpet Vine" has ". . . reddish flowers/That move like fingers and are deep as combs."
Colum continues to love the shade of red. "Stocks or Pinks or Gillyflowers" may be

> White as the wimple of a nun,
> Or pink as in an order changed.

Often women appear naturally among the flowers as in "Flowering Quince":

> —And you were there,
> With gifts, with graces, and with promises;

or in "Water Lilies" where the "gold and ivory" flowers, "the gauds of Africa," are lifted up by a Black girl who sells them. On the other hand, "Tiger Lilies" are "crookback knaves" and

> Perverters of the Lily's name
> With curld lips and tongues stuck out,
> The sooty spotted flowers of flame!

The final image of *Vegetable Kingdom* is not that of a flower, but of an old gardener, who, like a poet, dedicates his life to beauty. In "To Saint Fiacre, Patron of Gardens" Colum extols the cultivator, who, working alone, shapes order out of chaos, and is a nurturer to civilization:

> Old solitary man who wakens early
> To trim the hedges, raise the bended stalk,
> Cast weeds and slugs into the nether part,
> And clear the paths. O Fiacre,
> Still let there be a garden, not a wild!

The Vegetable Kingdom has neither the humor or the power of *Creatures,* but, nevertheless, it is a heart-warming creation of delicate poems, perhaps not a Royal Botanical Garden, but more than a mere cottage plot. Colum's love of life, his appreciation with advancing age of the beauty to be found in small things and little poems, and his keen eye for color, all blossom forth in *The Vegetable Kingdom,* creating a book for the gentle and unhurried to cherish.

Ten Poems (1957)

Ten Poems came out in Dublin in a limited edition of five hundred copies. Most of the poems had appeared in periodicals: the *Atlantic Monthly,* the *Dublin Magazine,* and the *Irish Times.* One of them, "Spinner's Song" was the result of Colum's combining "The Moon Cradle" from the first edition of *Wild Earth* with "Folding Hour" from *Poems.* The rest are newer works. The book is uneven. "Homage to Philip Sheridan," the Civil War Union general, finds Colum writing "under the Equestrian statue in Washington" and "laying a garland" to this soldier of Irish descent. The poem is melodramatic, pompous, hack, and out of place.

On the other hand, "The Book of Kells" is one of Colum's finest pieces, depicting the work of a medieval manuscript illuminator. He is describing his work, which he does *"in nomine Domini/Qui fecit caelum et terram."*

> First make a letter like a monument—
> ....
> Then, on a page made golden as the crown
> Of sainted man, a scripture you enscroll
> Blackly, firmly, with the quickened skill
> Lessoned by famous masters in our school,
> And with an ink whose lustre will keep fresh
> For fifty generations of our flesh.

The scribe's work, like his life, follows

> . . . a strict pattern:
> Illumination lighting interlace
> Of cirque and scroll, of panel and lattice.

Colum treats the scribe with great reverence and affection, for the poet saw himself not only as a medieval bard but, like the illuminator, a visual creator of flora and fauna. Additionally, Colum implies that in serving art the artist serves God too.

"A Road, A Garden and a Summer Evening" is a narrative in which the persona, a boy, describes his wonderment at all the new sights of the unfolding world including first seeing a man on a velocipede. Colum states in the headnote that he found his title and his idea for a poem, "Calen O Costure Me," in Shakespeare's *Henry V* where "a song is mentioned by a first line which Professor Gerard Murphy identifies as 'Cailin o chois tSuire me' meaning 'I am a girl from beside the Suir'—a popular song in assonantal metre, otherwise lost." In the poem a girl from Ireland is homesick in Elizabethan London where her kin, prisoners in the Tower of London, are hostages to peace in Ireland.

"The Hearthstone and the Loom" is a dialogue between two men, Maurice and Terence, who are looking into an abandoned house, and who recall the better days, in the past, which the house and the deceased inhabitant had known:

> Bread eaten without debt to harden it,
> Space in a house. . . .
> Work of the day that brings enough to keep
> Brave an innocence in its walks and ways,
> And festivals from time to time.

They and Colum would very much like Ireland to return to that halcyon time in the past when, they believe, a peasant utopia existed.

"The Basket-Maker" is another one of Colum's itinerant workers, a prince of the road, happy in his work and life, knowing he was of use to his fellowmen and women:

> I watched him go, his stock-in-trade upon him.
> "I travel Ireland's length and breadth," he said.
> There was dominion in the way he said it. . . .

"On Not Hearing the Birds Sing in Ireland" is a political lament which asks:

> What grim marauder made a spoil
> of bird and nestling,
> And left to us the songless woods,
> The songless fields of Eirinn?

"At Ferns Castle" is a song to an ancient ruin where the poet found "entrancement." The poem extols perception: "As syllables in holy words the blue was lined on high:/At Ferns Castle yesterday I looked upon the sky!"

"Egan O'Rahilly" sings of the old Irish bard, Aodhagán O Rathaille (1670–1726), who wrote beautiful, visionary poetry in which he saw Ireland as a lovely lady waiting for the return of her handsome lover from across the sea, perhaps standing for the Jacobite Pretender. Colum, or the persona, would like to believe in a messianic salvation for Ireland but, in the end, after the vision, there is only gloom and defeat.

In 1927 AE dedicated his new book of poems, *Voices of the Stones,* to his former protégé, Padraic Colum.[9] Having remained in Ireland, but in cosmopolitan Dublin and not in the countryside, AE said in the dedicating epistle:

> I made these verses in a rocky land,
> And I have named them Voices of the Stones,
> Although they do not keep that innocence
> Was shed on me when quiet made me kin
> To the cold immobile herd. All things have
>   changed.

AE's reference to the loss of an innocence which derived from silent observations of cattle, an image much closer to Colum's poetry than to AE's and thus a compliment to the younger writer, must have reminded Colum, now in busy New York City, of what he had left behind: rural Ireland, the source and inspiration of his art. Fortunately, there would be a returning at the time of departure.

Chapter Five
The Images of Departure

In the late 1950s from the age of seventy-five on, and after his wife's death, Padraic Colum began to look back and reminisce in thought and in verse on the many important people, the very shapers of modern Ireland, he had known in his long life. They were poets, scholars, soldiers, politicians, revolutionaries, actors, and clerics. All were gone. He alone had survived as if to tell their story to the young. In the process of this review Colum seems to achieve a renewal of vigor, a second blooming of poetic vitality. It began with new stirrings of nationalism and patriotism in him, a symbolic return to Ireland.

Irish Elegies (1958, 1961, 1963)

It was time for Colum to recognize cultural, political, and military heroes and also to say some thank yous to the dead. In Dublin in 1958 he published a first version of *Irish Elegies,* and added poems in 1961 and 1963. The Irish people embraced the book. The poems were not new. They were revisions.

Eleven poems appear in the 1963 edition. The first, "The Rebel, Roger Casement," underwent several versions from its origin in *Dramatic Legends,* until coming to rest in *Irish Elegies.* Colum lightened the poem by toning down its imagery. At the end, the English "die to dust." Phoenix-like, Casement's fate is "to die to fire."

Like "The Rebel, Roger Casement," "The Scholar, Kuno Meyer" is a lament employing the Gaelic cry of sorrow: "ochne, ochne." This second poem was first written in 1919 and was titled "The Rune-Master." For *Irish Elegies* Colum shortened and tightened the poem.

"The Painter, John Butler Yeats" was first written in 1924 and appeared in *Old Pastures* in 1930 as "In Memory of John Butler Yeats." The painter, William Butler Yeats's father, had painted Colum at age twenty-six in Dublin during the Abbey days. He left Ireland for a visit to New York in 1908, and as the Colums would also, he stayed there until he died in 1922 at eighty-three, his family in Dublin being unable to lure him back. Padraic and Mary were very fond of "Jack" Yeats all during his life in New York, and Colum's elegy to him is perhaps the most moving piece in the book. The charming poem as published in *Irish Elegies* contains an extra, unnecessary stanza. Colum had better ended with:

> Your words, your breath are gone!
> O uncaught spirit, we'll remember you
> By those remote and ever-flying birds
> Adown the Shannon's reach, or crying through
> The mist between Clew Bay and Dublin Bay!

And surely these beautiful words could serve as epitaph for the poet himself, lover of Ireland, lover of birds, author of *The Flying Swans,* and one also who would die in another country.

In "The Statesman, Arthur Griffith," Colum cut eight lines from the original poem entitled "Odysseus: In memory of Arthur Griffith" in *Old Pastures.* The poem is not improved by its cut because Colum omits a physical description of his old friend in *Irish Elegies.*

With only a few words changed "The Pilgrim, Thomas Hughes Kelly" is essentially the same poetic thank you to his old American friend and benefactor found in *Collected Poems.* Perhaps the tribute is somewhat out of place in *Irish Elegies.* However, the work is basically personal, not general, despite the fame of most of the subjects.

"The Artificer, James Joyce" was written within a short time after the novelist's death in 1941, but did not appear in a Colum collection until *Irish Elegies.* Colum has great sympathy for his tormented friend, who had "no refuge from afflictions/That bore on you and left you broken. . . ." Joyce is likened to both his hero, Stephen Dedalus, and to the great artificer of Greek mythology: "Daedalus! Has your flight ended so?" Typically, however, the heart of the poem, is a fond reminiscence:

> I looked back to the days of our young manhood,
> And saw you with the commons of the town
> Crossing the bridge, and you
> In odds of wearables, wittily worn,
> A yachtsman's cap to veer you to the seagulls,
> Our commons also, but your traffic
> Sombre: to sell your books upon the quay.

The poem ends with Colum's admission that he, like almost everyone else, had not at first recognized the great genius of Joyce, "the man with wings." "The Artificer, James Joyce" is one of Colum's first free-verse poems. It indicates that in his sixties at least, and later, he could move away from the more lyric forms for the right tone and effect. A traditional form, such as the ballad, for an elegy to a writer like James Joyce, a burster of language, would have been an unmitigated disaster.

"The Player, Dudley Digges" is the poem that appeared in *Collected Poems* as "The Dead Player: In Memory of Dudley Digges," almost doubled in length from eight to fourteen lines, and much improved by the addition, especially the line referring to the neoclassical tradition of striking a staff on the stage three times to announce the beginning of a play. In this case, however, it is death who is announced: "The solemn knocks are not for curtain's rise."

"The Poet, Seamus O'Sullivan," was written about 1958. Colum had been O'Sullivan's friend and fellow protégé of AE in the early days. O'Sullivan, who was born James Sullivan Starkey, turned out to be a minor poet, but also the founder of one of the most important Irish literary periodicals, the *Dublin Magazine*. Colum sweetly remembered the youthful fellow poet:

> And you would speak your poem as though abashed
> To bring a child so gentle through a crowd.
> But though averted, lightened were your eyes—

"The Magister, Monsignor Pádraig De Brún" is Colum's homage to a great Irish educator and translator of the classics into Irish. Monsignor De Brún, born Patrick Broune, died in 1960, so Colum's poem is among the latest in *Irish Elegies*. He laments not only the death of his scholar-friend but all the others of his brilliant generation:

> Since Yeats his eagle mind
> Resigned, our household grows
> Less and less genial:
> They leave who kept us proud.
> ....
> They leave us one by one!

This poem, written at about the age of seventy-nine, shows that Colum was remarkably sharp, as well as artistically flexible up to, and, as shall be shown, through the ninth decade of his life. As the Magister is master of knowledge, the poet seems to have conquered time.

Unlike most of the other poems in *Irish Elegies* "The Fenians, Allen, Larkin and O'Brien Hanged. . . ." is an elegy to a group of men who died long before Colum was born. Known to Irish history as the Manchester Martyrs, they were Fenians executed by the English in 1867 for the alleged murder of a police sergeant. The nationalistic poem is quite pedestrian. The last poem in the collection is "Ave Atque Vale" transferred intact from *Poems*.

By generally improving those elegies written earlier, by adding new pieces, and by bringing these poems together, Colum created something of a personal modern Irish history. He touched most aspects of Irish society and selected for eulogizing and inclusion a group of men whom he could simultaneously present in both a public and private fashion. Colum had hit upon an idea: he could offer poetry, biography, and even epic history by reordering, editing, and adding to his earlier poetry. His crowning achievement would be his next book of poetry in which he produced an epic of old Ireland through a new assembly of his lifetime's work.

The Poet's Circuits (1960)

Just as James Joyce's Dublin of Bloomsday, 16 June 1904, fortunately for literature, never left the novelist in his lifetime of exile, so also, though perhaps not as fortunately, Colum's turn-of-the-century Ireland never left the poet in his long years of exile, although his memory of it waxed and waned. It too was a fix in time and it ultimately produced *The Poet's Circuits*.

In preparing this volume Colum saw himself as a medieval Irish bard making his traditional rounds of the countryside:

In Medieval Ireland a poet from time to time crossed the boundry of the canton he had residence in and went through other cantons, giving recitals, meeting distinguished members of his guild, looking in on bardic schools, and closing with return to residence, bearing proper fees.[1]

The structure of *The Poet's Circuits* is centrifugal. The eight circuits are "The House," "Field and Road," "Things More Ancient," "The Glens," "The Town," "Women in the House," "People on the Road," and "Monuments." Colum says:

> The circuits begin in the house and with the entrance of traditional music and song, and then go to the field and the road along-side it. What is accessible from medieval life is encountered in the third circuit. The last circuit is not as plain as the others. The culture of the cottage has also gone into decay. Back further it is the Norman castle; it is the Irish Cashel; it is the bronze-age Dún; it is the unremembered cromlech. (*PC*, vi)

Although the idea of grouping poems around such places as houses, road, and field first occurred to Colum in 1922 when he edited *An Anthology of Irish Verse*, his organization here nevertheless is inspired. By rewriting and by careful selection and gathering he "added even greater significance to some of his best work."[2] Thus *The Poet's Circuits* remains, all in all, the best representation of his poetic achievement. He realized that if *Lowry Maen* had failed as an Irish saga, *The Poet's Circuits* would not. He states: "these poems of men and women make a . . . saga. It is as a saga and not as separate pieces that they should be presented" (*PC* v–vi). Colum also argues that "the poetic circuit is still a valid conception . . . because it assumes that a poet has a function, an obligation, a dedication, a definable territory to make his circuit through" (*PC* vi). Although almost eighty years old, Padraic Colum was still battling for a significant role for the poet in society.

The Poet's Circuits opens with a long, new "Fore-piece," and the reader is delightfully astonished at the power, vigor, and beauty of the fifteen-page, blank-verse poem, which contains echoes of William Wordsworth's *Prelude* in its story of youthful self-discovery, in its dealing with the mystery of creativity, and in its use of exquisite literal imagery.

"Fore-piece" is at least partially autobiographical. It is set in 1900, when, the persona says, "The Century that held my twenty years/ came to an end. . . ." He meets and is befriended by a peasant political activist named Owen Paralon, who also appeared in *Castle Conquer* (1923) and who may have been modeled on Colum's traveling, storytelling uncle, Micky Burns. The youth describes Owen's humble home as if it were a castle, thus implying, as Colum often does, the natural nobility of the peasant.

> And here was my host's house, Owen Paralon's.
> The walls were thick, as though some castle builder
> Had stooped to raise a house that would have only
> Bedrooms and attic over living room.

The house contains a silver cup, a chalice symbolic of its history and the honor of Ireland. Later it will serve for the investiture of the youth as poet.

After several experiences in coming to know the beauty and the sorrow of his native district, the youth writes a poem, takes it to Owen Paralon, and is recognized as the "poet of the place."And so the youth of "Fore-piece" becomes a lifelong poet, perhaps as Colum himself did around 1900. The lyrical, descriptive beauty of the poem must also be noted:

> Easter was betokened: half-grown lambs
> Beside their mothers in a rocky field;
> Black cattle making tracks
> Between the golden bushes of the whins;
> The crops enclosed with hedges, and the bog
> Rough with the heather that had shade of bloom.

"Fore-piece" is indeed a worthy introduction to Colum's finest poetry collection and the work by which he intended to be remembered as an Irish poet.

"Circuit One: The House" contains eight poems. Colum starts with the house because at the hearth, traditionally, the Irish poet sat and recited poetry to the family with their friends and servants all gathered about him. The first poem, "The Singers," is a rewrite and tightening of "Polonius and the Ballad Singers," originally in *Wild Earth* (1916). The new title makes much more sense since there was never a reference to "Polonius" in any of the versions of what was a three-part work: "Cruckaunfinn," "The Hawk-questing Maid," and "The Baltimore Exile."

The second poem in "Circuit One: The House" is "Storyteller."

This poem began as "The Man Who Dreamt of Treasures" in the original edition of *Wild Earth*. It became "The Ballad of Downal Baun" in the 1916 *Wild Earth, Poems,* and *Collected Poems.* "Poor Scholar," "Poet," "Old Soldier," and "Suiler" have had their long history of previous publication, while "Dreamer of the New Hearth" originally was part II of "The Furrow and the Hearth" in *Wild Earth* (1916). Finally, "After-piece" for this circuit is a combination of "The Moon Cradle" from the original *Wild Earth* and "Folding Hour" from *Poems.* It first appeared this way in *Ten Poems,* entitled "Spinner's Song."

"Circuit Two: Field and Road" contains ten poems. Quite naturally Colum leads off with one of his most famous poems "The Plougher." As he has taken us from the house to the field, his fine poem about the "earth-breaker" is a most appropriate choice to introduce what is perhaps the most poetically powerful of the circuits. "A Drover," "The Pedlar," "Branding Foals," "Knitters," are all old favorites and "After-piece" is essentially "The Terrible Robber Men" from the 1907 *Wild Earth.* "Sower" is a version of "Seed" from that first *Wild Earth* and "The Furrow and the Hearth" from the 1916 edition. The poem has been shortened and strengthened, with emphasis now on the man who is sowing. "The Pedlar" is essentially "Before the Fair," in *Poems,* with an additional stanza showing the pedlar dealing with the farmer's wife. "Man Who Gains a Charm" is a lengthened and reordered version of "The Charm" from *Collected Poems.*

The new pieces in "Circuit Two: Field and Road" are the third and fourth poems, "Hired Scytheman" and "Spadesman." Following "Plougher" and "Sower" they are clearly spin-off poems from the first two, which are among his earliest work. Colum needed more men in the field for this circuit. They are both strong poems worthy of their venerable predecessors. In "Hired Scythesman" an itinerant agricultural worker, somewhat reminiscent of Robert Frost's "Hired Man," teaches the persona, a lad, to reap:

> A CROOKED man stands in the gap beside a holly tree,
> And like a whetstone on a blade, his scraping words
> to me,
> 'The handles grip, you gawky lad, till swathe to
> swathe you lay,

> For Scythe must sweep from hedge to hedge to win
>   the spalpeen's pay.
>   From hedge to hedge, and quick at that,
>   To win the spalpeen's* pay.'
>
>   (*Spalpeen: a hired *scythesman*.)

The description of the man at work is precise and powerful:

> A stalwart man walks on the field, his arms have
>   steady swing,
> With flash of blade the grass is laid as even as
>   a string.

As the scythesman moves in his steady pace he calls to birds in the growing grain:

> Corncrake, 'twas often I heard you in the first
>   red streak of the day
> Me, with my melodies wasting, and you at the height
>   of your play
> And now I will narrow your meadow to win me the
>   spalpeen's pay.

"Hired Scythesman" leaves the reader with the feeling that he or she has encountered the genuine article, a proud Irish itinerant harvester of the past, one of the good earth's truly noble creatures in his natural setting. Remarkably, Colum is again able to describe and evoke the now nearly mythic figures of his childhood's landscape.

"Spadesman" is not quite as successful as "Hired Scythesman." For one, it is not as simple; Colum brings in a political element, the suggestion that fire rather than banners with words would solve the problem of the oppressed peasant. However, in the end he says:

> But let that be! I single out
> From folk of parish, odd and even
> The man upon the ridge alone
> The man with spade, the man hard-driven.

Together with "Hired Scythesman," however, "Spadesman" helps make "Circuit Two: Field and Road" fresh and vigorous. Furthermore these two new poems are evidence of Colum's renewed vitality as a poet.

The ten poems of "Circuit Three: Things More Ancient" take the reader back in time to both the days of early Irish civilization and early Christianity. "Queen Gormla" is one of the two heroic poems in the section. It is, with minor revisions "Queen Gormlai" in *Poems*. The other heroic piece is "Oisin Gormlai," another version of part of the Fenian legends. This time Colum is concerned with the valor of three Irish heroes, including Fian, in the *Fiana*, or stag hunt. One hero, the narrator, now an old man like Colum, sadly recalls the strength of youth and the living thoughts now gone.

"The Scribe" was "The Book of Kells" in *Ten Poems*, and "Saint Brendan" reappears from *Old Pastures*. The Bible is represented by "The Crucifixion" which is "Verses for Alfeo Faggi's Stations of the Cross" from *Poems* with a new title, and "Ishmael the Archer," a new, short verse about Ishmael's mourning for his mother, Hajar, adopted from "The Wayfayer" in the 1916 *Wild Earth*. Colum put "Crane," one of his old *Creatures* poems, in this circuit, but the remaining five poems are new to Colum's collected work. "Fore-piece" for "Circuit Three: Things More Ancient" is a long, blank-verse narrative about a man who came to an old Irish town on business. The place has an ancient cross and a cell where once a saint had sojourned. The visitor, a poet, is moved to rework his old material through the inspiration of the saint:

> . . . I went within
> The Saint's own cell, and, conscious of the light,
> I staid there, and reworded an old poem—
> A poem that had this light
> Moving across the countryside. . . .

Colum is writing about the possibility of artistic renewal, at any age, through the inspiration of worthy men or the intervention of God. His persona, returning to the Irish countryside, hearing the mother tongue, and standing before the great stone cross,

> . . . massive, circled
> Enscrolled and storied, something greatly wrought
> Out of that Ireland whose fortune was soon lost,

finds contentment and the ability to go on with life and work. This "Fore-piece" seems autobiographical too, but of an incident of his later life as compared to the youthful situation of the "Fore-piece" of *Poet's Circuits* itself.

"May Day" is a song to spring-time, to growing things, and to the beauty of budding life:

> And in the clear-skyed month
> Man comes into his own;
> The maiden in fair pride
> Buds and her beauty's
> known.

The literal imagery is delicate and Colum is superb in his simple evocation of the landscape:

> Bees load themselves from blooms;
> The kine go up the hill,
> Dry mud upon their flanks;
> The ants bear all they will.

The line "Dry mud upon their flanks" is a good example of Colum's precise artistry. Although a direct statement, the words cause the reader to focus on a part of the cattle, and see and feel their connection to the soil. The effect is achieved so efficiently, so subtly, that there is no sense of artistic contrivance and no jarring between the poet's thought and the reader's perception.

"Autumn" is a two-stanza poem, each stanza beginning with the line: "A good stay-at-home season is Autumn." Colum describes the rich world of maturing crops and then in the last line he selects the simplest, symbolic image: "And there by the rath the hazel nut drops from a load."

The "After-piece" of "Circuit Three: Things More Ancient" is a short poem about the wild birds that decorate the countryside: crows, haws, and "redbreasts." It is also about the gift of birdsong, "the high song that comes from the hedge." In a way it is almost an introduction to the next circuit.

"Circuit Four: The Glens" contains nine poems of which seven appeared in previous collections: "Sister's Lullaby," "Girls Spinning,"

"A Connachtman," "A Man Bereaved," "The Poor Girl's Meditation," "Crows," and "After-piece" which first was "Legend" in *Dramatic Legends*. The circuit opens with a four-stanza poem "Now,
Coming on Spring," which extols the season and tells of a person
from County Mayo who longs to return there to his village, Killeo-
dean. The last stanza introduces a new, historical figure in Colum's
poetry:

> And if Raftery stood in the midst of his people,
> Old age would go from him, and he'd step to his youth!

Antoine Raftery was a blind, uneducated, County Mayo folk poet
who lived from about 1784 to 1835 and whose poems survived in the
Irish oral tradition until collected and edited in 1903 by Douglas
Hyde. As an old Irish poet, living far from his homeland, Colum
clearly identified both with the homesick Mayo man and with Raftery. These last lines introduce the next poem in the circuit.

"Raftery" is an eight-stanza ballad in which, in the simplest, most
direct language, the blind poet is remembered more for his suffering
and loss than for his art.

> For what is fame beside a loss
> That every day can bruise?
> The shine upon the buckles broad
> Of a worn pair of shoes.

"Circuit Five: The Town" contains ten poems. Nine of them, "The
Chapel Yard," which was "The Saint" in *Poems* and which received an
additional stanza; "The Market Place," which was "A Basket Maker"
in *Ten Poems*; "Honey-Seller" and "The Toy Maker" which were part
of "Reminiscence" in *Dramatic Legends*; "Asses," "Tin Whistle
Player," "Ballad-Maker," "Fox," and "After-piece," originally "She
Moved Through the Fair," had been previously published and have
undergone no changes or only minor ones. The one new poem in
"Circuit Five: The Town" is an excellent example of Colum's continued ability to present fascinating psychological profiles, in which,
through monologues, the true nature of the speaker on the subject is
revealed, sometimes without the persona's intention.

"Old Woman Selling Ducks" is the portrait of a poor woman who must sell her four beloved pet ducks. The "old body" and the ducks are both terrified:

> From each end of the basket, too frightened to quack,
> A duck sticks a beak,
> And frightened is she, the old body who'd sell them,
> And hardly will speak:
> As she trudges along with her ducks, each as thin
> As the water-hen!

Although the portrait verges on sentimentality, it appropriately stops short of bathos, leaving us with just the right amount of emotion. We sorrow for human and animal, who after all, share a common fate. The focus is correctly on the fear, not the situation. Colum still celebrates the poor, the lame, the blind, the downtrodden.

"Circuit Six: Women in the House" contains eleven poems, nine of which were previously published in collection and received only minor emendations in *The Poet's Circuits*. "Women in the Hearth" was "Interior" in *Poems*, "The Mountain Thrush" was a part of "Reminiscence" in *Dramatic Legends* and "After-piece" was enlarged from "Woodbine" in *Old Pastures*. The other reprints are "Girls Spinning," "Across the Door," "Cradle Song," "No Child," "Dermott Donn Macmorna," and "Old Woman of the Roads." The new poems are "Saint Anne's Feast Day" and "The Call for the Bride."

"Saint Anne's Feast Day" is a remembrance of "A day of distant reverence." The persona recalls the young women of his youth, "Rose, Maurya, Anne, Shevaun," and seems to hear them tell the chapters of their lives as "Maid, wife, or grandmother." This sedate poem is contrasted by the piece that follows, as if the persona, in a dream, has moved from remembering his youth, to participating, once more a young man, in the marriage game.

"The Call for the Bride" is collected in *Poet's Circuits* for the first time, although Colum said he had begun to work on the poem years before.[3] It is a very funny dramatic dialogue between an angry mother who wants to thwart her daughter's suitor and the daughter who not only wants the suitor but tries to obtain a large dowry, too:

> Oh, mother sell all that you have to your name,
> To give me a dowry to equal my fame—

> Sell the cow, and the sow, and the gander that's lame,
> And the sack of black wool in the corner!

The girl is not only vain but is also quite naive in thinking that an Irish peasant woman would sell everything for a daughter's dowry, especially when she has another daughter.

In the beginning the mother's outraged greeting of the suitor and his friends at her door is especially vivid and delightful:

> For a bride you have come! It is with a full score
> Of rake-hell rapscallions you'd fill up my door,
> With a drum to your tail and a fiddle before,
> And a bag-piper playing all through ye?
>
> My faith! Do you think that a shy little maid
> Would lift up her head before such a brigade,
> When an arm round her waist would make her afraid?
> By my hand! She has gone from my keeping.
>
> Through the gap in the hedges away she has run;
> Like the partridge across the wide stubble she's gone,
> And here I am, here I am, here I'm alone
> With no daughter to give any comer!

Of course, the mother is lying, and she's caught, for the girl enters immediately:

> Well here she is back! I declare she has come
> Like the cat to the cradle. . . .

The comedic situation of "The Call for the Bride" shows that Colum, even in his poetry, could call upon his earlier talents in the drama to create quick expositions, brief but fast plots, and fine characterization with very few pen strokes.

"Circuit Seven: People on the Road" contains nine poems of which six were collected previously: "The Beggar's Child," "The Toy-Maker," "Man with Grinding-Wheel," which was "Blades" in *Old Pastures*; "A Hundred Men Think I am theirs," which was "An Drinaun Donn" in the 1916 *Wild Earth*; "Nor Right, Nor Left, Nor Any Road," which was first "A Rann of Exile" in the original *Wild Earth*;

and "Man Out of Bounds" which was first a part of "Reminiscence"
in *Dramatic Legends*. The new poems are "Spadesmen," "I went out in
the evening," and "Wanderer's Song," the after-piece for the circuit.

"Spadesmen" again introduces to Colum's readers the road people
of whom the poet was so fond. In a dialogue between a spadesman
and a scholar "the men and women of no fixed abode" are character-
ized by the former, who tends to judge people according to how close
their occupations bring them to the breaking of the soil. Tinkers, for
example, ". . . have no friendliness for field or house/They have a
curse for all who own a roof."

Both the spadesman and Colum understand hard work:

> 'Twas a long day's digging, and by rain-drenched men,
> Or sweating men, and at the end of it,
> The men could sleep on harrows.

"Spadesmen" reminds the reader of Colum's early love for the Irish
road and the pageant of travelers that he first experienced in childhood and first wrote about in *The Road Round Ireland* (1926).

"I went out in the evening" is a four-stanza romantic ballad in
which, one evening, a young man visits his sweetheart's cottage unexpectedly, only to see through her window that she is entertaining
another. Her freedom is an anathema to him and he despairs:

> My love she is courteous and handsome and tall;
> For wit and behavior she's foremost of them all!
> She says she is no way bound, that with me she'll go free,
> But my love has too many lovers to have any love for me!

The lilting song is direct and charming. It exhibits the values and
the feelings of the agrarian Ireland of Colum's youth. Its work is to
evoke nostalgia for a simple, pastoral life, indeed a life that may only
have existed in the minds of poets looking back on a romanticized
past through misty lenses.

"After—piece—Wanderer's Song" is a poem to the star Betelgeuse.
It is a star for exiles, a reminder of distance and time left behind. In
the end, the constant star helps the persona to "know what dust my
bone and flesh will be." Betelgeuse is thus a star for "people on the
road."

"Circuit Eight: Monuments" contains fourteen poems of lament for the Ireland of the past, beginning with the country of Colum's youth and going back to the Ireland of the Middle Ages. They represent his most nationalistic statement in *Poet's Circuits*. However, it must be pointed out that Colum's nationalism did not include any illusions about the possibility of a returning to an ancient heroic Ireland or that a heroic age for Ireland might come again. In this regard he differed significantly from his old mentor, AE, and from Yeats.[4]

All the poems in "Circuit Eight: Monuments," however, were collected earlier. "The Deer of Ireland," "The Big House," and "Jacobite Song" were all first collected as untitled pieces in the "Reminiscence" section of *Dramatic Legends*. "Fern's Castle" came out of *Ten Poems* as did "On Not Hearing the Birds Sing" which originally was titled, "On Not Hearing the Birds Sing in Ireland" and "The Hearthstone and the Loom" to which Colum added twenty-three lines. "Egan O'Rahilly's Vision" was "Egan O'Rahilly" in *Ten Poems*. "Pierce Ferriter to Meg Russell" was "Shall I Go Bound and You Go Free?" in *Dramatic Legends*. Also, "After-piece," "Below There Are White-Faced Throngs" was "To a Poet" in *Dramatic Legends* to which Colum added a new stanza. "O Woman Shapely as a Swan" was "I Shall not Die for Thee" in the 1916 *Wild Earth*. From *Old Pastures* came "Fourteenth-Century Lament" which originally was titled "Breffne Caoine," and "Cashel" which was first called "At Cashel." "The Cromlech" is a section of *The Story of Lowry Maen*. Lastly, "The Dún" began as "For Morfydd" in the 1916 *Wild Earth*, was slightly revised in the "Reminiscence" in *Dramatic Legends*, and rewritten to make it less sentimental and more of a lament in *Poet's Circuits*. The poem in "Reminiscence" ends joyously and with hope:

> I bring you; you bring me again, the love,
> the triumph, the strife!

In *Poet's Circuits* it ends forlornly:

> The rule and the treasure are gone, but the story lives
> like the leaves,
> The story I told of our loves that was writ on the
> poet's staves.

Poet's Circuit is Colum's ultimate achievement in poetry. He successfully attempted to create a unified framework for his lifetime's poetry and to convert a mass of simple and beautiful lyrics into an epic both historical and social. The "small art" of the ballad and the dramatic monologue takes on significant proportions when displayed as of a whole cloth. Colum's late inspiration to select, reorganize, edit, and revise his canon was indeed a stroke of genius. *Poet's Circuit* has become and probably will remain a significant part of modern Irish literature.

Images of Departure (1969)

Padraic Colum published one of his finest books at the age of eighty-seven. *Images of Departure* contains twenty poems in which he remembers his dead wife with great fondness and in which he says farewell to Ireland and long life. The poems are both very personal and at the same time universal. In several Colum substitutes himself, an old man full of sharp memories, for such personae as drovers and spadesmen. One poem, "The Book of Kells" is again reprinted from *Ten Poems*. The first piece in the collection, the title poem, "Images of Departure," is preceded by a long head note in which Colum says:

The Images of Departure in this poem are taken from a seventeenth-century Gaelic poem by Thomas Costello addressed to Una MacDermott, and from Orpheus and Eurydice, a statue by John Hughes in the Modern Art Gallery in Dublin. In the first the departure is in anger, in the second it is in reconciliation.

In the first half of the poem the persona, and in this case it is surely Colum, has returned to Dublin to see once more the old row houses:

>   Each with a fanlight ribbed above the door,
>   And (emblem of persistence it could be),
>   A knocker rounded as an iron wreath.

He remembers his wife when she was a young woman and living in a Dublin lodge:

> "And is there one, a student, living here?"
> (The words recurring and the heart-beats, too)
> ....
> No girl will rise from her deep arm-chair
> And make a jest of greeting; I look towards
> Electric glare instead of oil-lamp's glow.

Quickly the poet turns to the poem "Costello/Bestowed upon MacDermott's downcast child."

In the second half of "Images of Departure" Colum sees in the sculptor John Hughes's statue of Orpheus and Eurydice an emblem in eternal stone of his lifelong love for Molly, his wife.

> They have not aged, this pair; they well remember
> The eagerness of first companionship,
> The dreams, the ardors, and the prophecies.

There is peace for the poet in the thought that his love will, like the statue, live on, not through sculpture but with words. "Images of Departure" is one of Colum's most inwardly expressive poems, a song of praise to the solace of memory.

> The gazers move with recognitions due
> To names and figures that are trophies here:
> I stand before your marble pair, John Hughes,
>
> To know that, like a bird down on a branch
> Stray, unbeckoned, out of a wide sky
> Has come to them the moment of accord.

Another poem in which his remembered love for Molly plays a part is "Expecting No One." In this poem Colum's deep loneliness is manifested as he leans upon the ledge of a bridge:

> . . . expecting no one
> From north or south, a pilgrim who is mindful
> Of all he left behind, and mindful, too,
> Of disrepair in all he has come back to.

There is little relief in this poem for the lost love of a lifetime. The pain and the grief may be greatest for the old, who have so little

chance to find love again. In the end, and near to his departure from
the world he has known for so long and enjoyed as much, the persona
stands watching "seagulls making their disordered flight,/Expecting
no one from the south or north."

Three poems in *Images of Departure* seem to allude to Colum's long-
dead mother. They are "After Speaking of One Who Died a Long
Time Before," "Forget Me Nots," and "Near Legend." The first is a
poem of regret for the inadequacies of Ireland before independence.
The poet deplores the poverty and the lack of dreams in the lives of
those like his mother who lived out their time in the nineteenth century. He would:

> . . . speak of all she lost in her life's decades.
> "She should have had," you said, touched by what held me
> "The simple things that we will always have."

Surrounded by his beloved flowers, tulips and asphodels and others, the poet recalls in "Forget Me Nots" flowers used in an old-fashioned manner, as his mother might have done:

> And I had seen their semblance stitched upon
> A brim of hat by one who scarcely knew
> A holiday from year's end to year's end. . . .

In "New Legend" Colum alludes directly to his mother, when an
itinerant worker chops firewood for her, and nobly, as Colum would
have put it, does not accept a gift in payment. The event is seen
through the eyes of childhood:

> We stood by and watched the stranger.
> "Now," he said when ceased the onset,
> "You have firewood till nigh Christmas."
> She came to herself, our mother,
> Who had stood there like a statue.
> Lifting pot that had geranium
> In full bloom, she brought it to him
> As thank-offer for his labour,
> "No," he said, "I take no payment,
> What my adze can do is given."

Colum remains true to his belief in the dignity of the peasant and the
greatness of those who are simple and generous.

In *Images of Departure* Colum brings back his favorite tree in "Sleep and the Laburnam Tree" in which the persona asks for sleep to help him endure loneliness and despair. The tree's goldness becomes a desired "offering to the obscure."

"In Saint Stephen's Green," that central place in Colum's old Dublin, the poet finds

> . . . on the tree above
> A nest from seasons gone
> That keeps in spite of all that blew
> A lone, wild homeliness.

Can it not but remind him of himself?

"Day's End" is about an old poet imitating an old woman calling her chickens. The poet is trying to call back the days of his life, which, like stolen chickens, are now gone:

> Evenings ten thousand
> Were here and are gone,
> Foxes that bear off
> This one and that one.
> "They're out," says the poet,
> "Like the flame of the rush-
> Candle; they're gone
> Like a girl's first blush."

The analogy holds up. A poet's memory is his stock as a peasant's fowls are hers. Loss is loss. And in the end life is loss too. "Day's End" indicates a fresh new sublety to Colum's poetry, the delightful surprise of *Images of Departure*.

"In the Caribbean" is a slight piece, two stanzas recalling Ireland from the Caribbean Sea. "Before a Row of Votive Candles" finds the persona seeking hope and inspiration in the good office of prayer candles. "Sean O'Dwyer A Gleanna" laments the fall of a hero at the Battle of the Boyne. "Judgement" is a cryptic, personal poem about loved ones meeting after Judgement Day.

"Name and Legend" is a memory piece in which the poet hopes that someone will

> Dream of me there in stirless air,
> Beyond the seagull's range,
> Above enshadowed beings we name
> Time and Loss and Change.

Colum presents an old-fashioned ballad about the madness of the creative process in "Then I Was Mad." In "The Dying Gaul" the poet writes about the famous statue as he had done previously in *The Flying Swans*. He offers a tribute "To Dame Margot Fonteyn," the great ballet dancer. The "Wild Duck" presents Colum with "An image . . . to hearten all my ways." In "Australian Tree" he finds another tree to love and glorify, the flame tree with "The red that's forged to flame."

"Discovery" finds the persona lying "upon a bank of grass / In idleness." He observes the teeming life in the grass and reflects:

> Years have gone by like flight of drones,
> Droning away. Still, as I chance
> On lawn or sward, I bend my wits
> To hear a murmur, rumour near,
> And be again discoverer!

"Discovery" summarizes Colum's lifelong adventure as a discoverer of life, and a recorder of the beauty and the strength of the smaller, humbler things.

Note must be taken of Colum's particular use of bird imagery in *Images of Departure*. Domestic birds, game fowl, birds of flight, exotic birds, all caught his attention and served to symbolize, in this book particularly, both the beautiful, graceful presence of nature and the passage of a life. In "Images of Departure" peace is "a bird down on a branch." Magpies stand for repair and renewal in "In Saint Stephen's Green." "Seagulls fly up from the darkened river" in "Expecting No One." "Their flight disordered—there is emblem here." The seagulls, like the old poet, also expect "no one from the south or north."

Seagulls and swifts fly in "Name and Legend," the former around earthly objects, while the latter like souls, "glide . . . until the vault of sky they reach." The "Wild Duck" symbolizes independence and the corncrake represents survival in "Near Legend." There are other aviary images in *Images of Departure*. Perhaps the image of the bird departing, its song growing softer in the distance, is Colum's own final and ultimate image of his departure from love and from life.

Images of Departure is a gracious and beautiful farewell to art and life. The modest, objective, lyric poet finally moved to the center stage of his work. The book leaves behind an image of a very old artist, clear of thought, the last survivor of his great time, remembering love and friendship as he faces death with some sadness and much hope.

Padraic Colum was a unique poet. He went his own way. He wrote poetry in the middle of the twentieth century the way he had learned it at the end of the nineteenth century and he did so without apology. He enjoyed creativity and he enjoyed *being* a poet, an Irish poet. He incorporated ancient Gaelic subjects and form into the mainstream of English poetry. In a sense, he was a culture translator and a reconciler of antagonistic traditions. Both Irish culture and English-language poetry are richer for the poetry of Padraic Colum. It is unfortunate that his work never received the critical attention it deserved.

Chapter Six

The Man of Letters: Fiction, Biography, and Essays

Padraic Colum tried his hand at everything there is to do as a writer. In the realm of prose he wrote two well-received novels, many short stories, two important biographies, four travel essay books, almost innumerable introductions and pieces for periodicals, as well as some twenty-five books of children's literature and folklore (to be examined in the next chapter). His ability and success in nondramatic prose offers more evidence of his overall skill as a writer.

It is safe to say that almost all of Colum's prose, not for children, takes Ireland as its subject. The novels and the stories have Irish settings, the biographies are on Irish subjects, and the travel essays are about Irish life. Beginning as interpretations of Irish culture and values to Americans, and to some extent the English, Colum's prose, particularly his novels, is now published and widely read in Ireland. The younger generations of Irish men and women have turned to Colum to have their own cultural history explained to them.

Colum's prose style is constant through almost seventy years of writing. He favors direct declarative sentences, simple or compound rather than complex; the present tense, usually third-person narration; sparse, precise symbols sparingly used; and literal rather than figurative imagery. His dialogue is realistic, never "stage Irish." It tends to shorter exchanges rather than long, long monologues which he saves for special, highly dramatic situations. Whenever possible and artistically called for, Colum uses syntax as derived from the Gaelic, strained through the Anglo-Irish dialect. Lastly, he takes special care with description of Irish locales, almost to a fault in fact, because the reader occasionally senses that the magic of the language has charmed the author into describing what is in his heart rather than what his eye has seen. But then, Padraic Colum wrote most of his "Irish" prose in America and from memory.

The Novels

Save for the futility of it, a critic may be tempted to wish that Colum had written more novels. Clearly he saw his work as a novelist as secondary to his work as a poet, yet, like his poetry, his prose in his two novels, *Castle Conquer* (1923) and *The Flying Swans* (1957), has a unique combination of qualities: a highly evocative power of Irish landscape description, an ability to weave a sense of mysticism into a stream of words, and great skill in providing rich, credible detail of Irish peasant life in the late nineteenth century. The weaknesses in Colum's prose in his novels are his tendency occasionally to overuse symbols, to wander sometimes from the central narrative into storytelling as in the children's books, and, especially in *Castle Conquer*, to be somewhat heavy-handed in anti-English propaganda.

Castle Conquer is an idyllic, poetic romance, sometimes humorous and sometimes full of pathos, set in the 1870–1880 period of Irish history in which the seeds of the later, successful Irish Revolution were sown. The hero of *Castle Conquer* is Francis Gillis, a young Irishman who received an education for the priesthood in Spain but did not take orders. Having returned to his native land, he is treated as something of a lunatic for not having become a priest. The peasants consider him a "spoilt priest." Eventually, however, he overcomes their suspicions and becomes a leader in an early, abortive republican movement. Clearly, his calling is for nationalism, not religion.

After his return from Spain, Gillis becomes a farmhand on the small holding of Honor Paralon, a woman with enough greed for land to betray her fellow peasants. Honor has two daughters, Brighid and Oona; the former, a beautiful young girl, wins Gillis's heart. Realizing the evils that derive from the Anglo-Irish-ruled Castle Conquer, symbolic of English control of Ireland, Gillis joins the ineffective revolutionaries who are trying to redress those wrongs experienced by the peasantry. Ordered to join the British army in order to subvert the enlisted Irish soldiers, he binds Brighid to himself in a secret troth. They consider themselves married, hoping eventually to obtain Honor Paralon's consent.

After unsuccessfully defending a starving peasant about to be evicted from his small holding, Gillis is accused of shooting to death a landlord's agent.

In fact, while the crime was occurring, Francis and Brighid were consummating their love, and in order to save his life at the trial she must endure public disgrace by confessing that they had slept together without benefit of clergy. He is sentenced to five years' imprisonment for conspiracy, but pardoned by a new English government after two years. They are married and the story comes to an end except for an epilogue in which, forty years later, Gillis helps his son who is a commander of Irish revolutionary troops, and with whom he experiences the founding of the Irish Free State.

Castle Conquer has many excellent sections. The view of the appalling Irish poverty of the last century is grimly moving. The struggle of good and decent peasants against the grinding landlords, forever foreclosing, forever selling off at auction the peasant's few and pitiful livestock, forever gouging rents almost out of human flesh, provokes frustration and anger in the reader. The panorama of the Irish countryside with its dirty beggars, pipers, shopkeepers, constabulary, storytellers, handsome and hopeful young people, fields and cabins, physical beauty, and historical richness is hauntingly drawn. The genius of the book is the sense of time and place.

Early in the book Gillis is transfixed by what his ancestor, the chieftain O'Failey, had done once to drive the Anglo-Normans out of Castle Conquer.[1] Colum argues for the need of a people continually to recall their past in order to find motivation and courage for action in the future.

As always, Colum treats the Irish peasantry with great dignity. It is, after all, his special reversal of order. It is they, not the Anglo-Irish gentry, who are the true nobility of Ireland:

The moment that Sir John Seagrave's agent was to be brought into the house the peasants became at once nobles: they listened to him with dignity; they treated him with consideration, and it was all done as if a whole stately tradition was embodied in the brother and sister and the two young girls. Owen gave him a dignified message for Sir John Seagrave; he came with the departing guest; he held his horse while he mounted; he waited while he rode down the bohereen. And so, as between Owen Paralon and the owner of a Cahirmoy, the last word was with Owen Paralon. (*CC*, 93)

Castle Conquer abounds with vivid descriptions, opportunities for Colum to use his poetic powers, as when a group of agricultural workers rent and survey the land:

> The bog, as they saw it from where they sat, was something of a wilderness, and something of a garden, and something of a work-field. Between the heather and the blue sky the larks sang. There were thick growths of heather, level spaces of black bog-soil, pits filled with black water, clumps of brown turf that had been cut out of the soil and of heavier black turf that had been taken out of the pits; there was the *ceanavaun*, or bog-cotton, weakly and tall, with heads that seemed white as sugar drops above the black soil or against the black turf clumps; there was the bog-myrtle with the sunlight on its leaves; there were bunches of shining grasses and here and there odd and little flowers; trees had been dug out of the bog-soil; whitened now they looked like heaps of dried bones. All around, and running into the bog that was cut and level, the heather made a wilderness. (*CC*, 184–85)

Colum loves to relate the ancient customs and traditions of Ireland. The celebration of the Feast of Saint Brighid is lovingly described (*CC*, 258).

The love affair between Francis and Brighid is delicately drawn. The modern reader will find it somewhat old-fashioned in its verbal passion but lack of physical contact until the one, fateful act of love, but Colum's writing is realistic both for the era he wrote of and the time he wrote in. The reader is charmed and touched by the lovers and relates to them.

Finally, Colum's characters in *Castle Conquer* are credible. Gillis is a courageous young man, yet he is not a super-hero; he makes errors of judgment and his strength has limitations. Brighid, although very young and innocent, nevertheless is able to muster great courage to help the man she loves. Other characters, from the grasping mother, ironically named Honour, to the hunchbacked land agent Jonathan Woulfe, are convincingly created. *Castle Conquer* was a fine start for Padraic Colum in the novel form. It is perhaps unfortunate that he waited thirty-four years to publish a second novel for adult readers despite the fact that *Castle Conquer* was favorably reviewed.

The Flying Swans (1957), Colum's epic-length novel of 538 pages, obviously was only a part of what the author planned as a much longer story, perhaps a trilogy.[2] Events are foreshadowed, such as a sojourn in Vienna, which do not have time to occur, and the hero, Ulick, Gaelic for Ulysses, has no chance as yet to venture forth. Perhaps a somewhat indifferent reception by most major literary critics caused Colum to lose interest in the project in which he had invested ten years of work, and which the *Dial*, a prestigious literary journal, had published in part while Colum was still engaged in writing it.

The Flying Swans is a *Bildungsroman* telling the story of Ulick O'Rehill from his birth to early manhood. His father, Robert O'Rehill, is a romantic, unrealistic, peripatetic, anti-clerical dreamer, who dreams of ancestral aristocratic glory, but is a failure in life. He marries a beautiful peasant girl, but he considers her beneath him. He sires two sons, Ulick and Breasal, then leaves for America falsely claiming that Breasal is not his child. He returns near the end of the book to be reconciled with his two motherless sons.

Ulick, a would-be artist, having first lost his father and then rejecting the returned exile, continually finds father figures among relatives and friends. Particularly, he develops a love-hate relationship with the watchmaker and gambler, Anthony Duineen, a long-time friend and advisor of Ulick's mother. Thus the plot of *The Flying Swans* is essentially a boy's quest to find himself, to understand the complex, impoverished adult world around him, to reconcile himself with his heritage, and to attain manhood.

The novel's simple plot gives Colum a framework on which to hang a gallery of memorable nineteenth-century Irish types. Essentially, *The Flying Swans* is a book of portraits as seen through the developing perceptions of a sensitive, growing, and maturing youth. By far the most interesting of the portraits is that of the father, Robert O'Rehill. He is dream-tortured and betrayed by his obsession with his disinherited Catholic aristocratic background. He evidences the folly of living in the romantic past. Beset by rejections and financial loss, he is unfaithful to his wife, fathers an illegitimate child with a cousin, engages in a Raskolnikov kind of relationship with a prostitute, goes to prison for assault, runs away to America to find his fortune, fails, and secretly returns; and finally becomes a mystical, pagan hermit. When toward the end of the book Robert is confronted by his son, Ulick, he offers his newfound "philosophy." He is a Manichean and a devotee of the power of darkness.[3] Needless to say, Ulick rejects his father's heresy. The son will remain with the Christian god in the Catholic Church.

Saba, Ulick's mother, is a delicate portrait of loveliness and self-sacrifice and is, perhaps, based on Colum's remembrance of his own mother who died when the poet was sixteen, and whose husband left for America and returned empty-handed. From the beginning she is out of place as the wife of a middle-class aspirant to upper levels of society. Saba cannot pretend to be what she is not and as a result loses the respect of her servants (*FS*, 47). After a short unhappy life of struggle and poverty she dies, mercifully, at peace. Even in her dying Colum treats Saba with the greatest of care and tenderness (*FS*, 353). She is a magnificent Irish woman.

Other wonderfully drawn characters include Ulick's maternal grandfather, Breasal O'Breasal; Anthony Duineen; Ulick's brother, Breasal; the tinkers Lem and Sal Grabbit who smack of Dickens; Nan the prostitute; Ulick's several girlfriends; and many, many others. Old, pre-revolutionary Ireland's lost people of the farm, the village, and the road are all preserved in *The Flying Swans*, a title symbolic of both freedom and passing beauty.

The Flying Swans moves very slowly and requires much patience on the reader's part. One needs to relish the description of place and the sense of time in the novel for they really are the "heroes" of *The Flying Swans*. In a sense this book is like Isaac Bashevis Singer's novels of old Jewish life in Poland: *The Manor, The Estate,* and *The Family Moskat,* works of character and milieu set in older worlds among people of great historical tradition. Although Colum is by no means the consummate novelist Singer is, nevertheless, he too achieves, like Singer, a considerable measure of success in juxtaposing struggling humanity oppressed by foreign or alien masters, yet ever persevering and enduring.

Colum uses *The Flying Swans* to point out the difficulty of achieving manhood in an impoverished and subjected land. The path of survival requires responsibility for others and thus Ulick takes responsibility for his brother; and it requires a degree of acceptance of one's fate, which Ulick fulfills in his tortured relationship with his father and with his work as a stonecutter, the latter representing a rejection of vain, genealogical day-dreaming for honest, hard work.

Lastly, a salient feature of this neglected novel is Colum's skilled use of the cadence and images of the Irish-English dialect of the last half of the nineteenth century. The piety of the people is expressed in such phrases as "God never closed one door but he opened another."

A stingy couple is described: "They wouldn't let you have daylight if they could keep it from you." The book abounds with memorable descriptions and phrases. Thus *The Flying Swans* is a grand mural of old Ireland, painted in Irish words by a self-exiled survivor of that time with a long memory and a loving heart, yet an unfinished work with promise unfulfilled.

Short Stories

Padraic Colum wrote short stories continually during his entire writing career. Some of these stories were for adult readers and they appeared in various periodicals in Ireland and in America; others were for children and they came out in Colum's children's books and in periodicals for children. Colum published two collections of adult stories, *Studies* (1907) and *Three Men* (1930). These books are representative of his work in this genre, for they employ the satire, realism, and romanticism found generally in his stories.

Studies contains the dramatic narrative discussed in chapter two and two stories, "Eilis: A Woman's Story" and "The Flute Player's Story." Eilis is an old Irish woman who can still speak Gaelic. She recalls the hard life of her childhood and the death of her father after his mistreatment by the landlord:

> In a while it came to the priest's turn, and my father was anointed. I said to my man: "If my father is to die, I would like him to die under our roof." Michael stood up, the man who never denied me anything, and he went to the door. Something put it into my mind to go over to him again, "It will bring a blessing on our children," I said. He went out.
>
> In a while Michael was back. He carried my father across the fields. "Sister," said he (he always called me sister), "wipe the sweat off my face." My father was on his back, and I wiped the sweat off my man's face. We put my father to bed, and he died in the night.[4]

Never is Colum's prose more forceful and direct than in this story. The heart of the piece concerns Eilis's young love for someone other than her betrothed and her inability, despite prayer, to cross a ditch and reach her lover's arms to consummate the affair and prevent herself from marrying the unromantic middle-class man that was her father's choice. From the perspective of old age, however, when asked by the narrator if she has regrets, she admits that she liked her husband's voice after all.

Part of the charm of this story is the way Colum frames it by having his narrator, a young man like himself, visit the kitchen where old Eilis is knitting. The narrator first joins with Eilis in some good-natured banter and then extracts her story, made more romantic by the scrim of sixty or more years. The double narration adds charm and deep perspective to a very moving story.

"The Flute Player's Story" is a tragedy of love. The narrator is walking a road in Connemara when he comes across a drunken derelict being sent on his way by a policeman who does not arrest the drunk because he is a flute player, and thus a privileged artist. (*St,* 38–40) Later, the narrator meets the flute player again and their conversation is interrupted by a passing, broken-down circus wagon pulled by one sick, old horse. On board are a homely couple, fallen on hard times. They know the flute player. The woman, now heavy and unattractive, was once the young widow with whom the flute player was in love, and whom he lost to the man with her. The victorious suitor of years ago taunts the musician when he recognizes his old rival and when his wife tries to be civil to the flute player. The van moves on with mutual insults between the two men. Then the fat, bald, ugly, drunken musician tells the story of his lost love to the narrator. It is a sad tale of rivalry and misunderstanding. The flute player, good with the widow's circus horses, could not understand how the young widow could prefer a younger, perhaps more handsome but less able man to himself. He knew that marriage to his rival would ruin the widow and he was right. Still she seems happy while his life is now a drunken shambles.

Colum makes no moral judgment. The story speaks for itself. The reader is given the opportunity to see the flute player as he may have looked when young, to consider the motivation of the widow, to try to understand how love may lead to choices clearly not in the best interest of the people involved, and to realize that, regardless of choice, lovers grow old and the world turns shabby. The overall effect of the excellent story is one of delicate nostalgia and great reader satisfaction in that he or she is able to participate in the process of the story, helping to "color in" the characters with his or her own perspective and judgment.

Three Men (1930) contains one long, amusing story satirizing the psuedo-intellectuals of the imaginary Eblana Literary Society. There is much status in being invited to membership in the society but, in fact, the members are generally unworthy. They read interminably long and absurd papers to each other and they physically battle with each other too. Colum is attacking the critics and scholars of the Irish Renaissance as well as academic pretension everywhere. The story, published in a limited 500-copy edition, is deserving of a wider audience than it has received. It is not as esoteric as Colum apparently thought it was.

Most of Padraic Colum's short stories for adult readers are not accessible to the general reading public. They are scattered about the world of back-issue publications, appearing in such diverse and distant periodicals as the *United Irishman* and the *New Yorker*. An anthology of selected stories by Colum would be a valuable and delightful addition to Irish literature.

Biography

Although Padraic Colum had worked on *Ourselves Alone: The Story of Arthur Griffith and the Origin of the Irish Free State* (1959), long before he began working on *Our Friend James Joyce* (1958), it is the latter that first appeared in print. In fact it was Molly who had received the contract for a book on Joyce.[5] The project particularly delighted her, but her health was not up to it. Padraic began helping her with the book. The last morning of her life found her working on the book. After her death Colum continued the project, using her notes for much of that part of *Our Friend James Joyce* that is preceded by her name. However, at least two-thirds of the book is his effort, although it is published as written by Mary and Padraic Colum. In a prefatory note Colum explains:

The inspiration for *Our Friend James Joyce* came from Mary Colum and the shape of the narrative was planned by her. Illness prevented her from writing as many chapters as she intended; however, by discussing the whole work with me, by recalling situations, by enlivening the recollections that we both could draw on, she, to a large extent, carried through what she initiated.[6]

As always, Colum was generous.

Our Friend James Joyce is not an attempt at yet another life of Joyce. The Colums merely wanted to offer their personal experiences with Joyce and his family. Additionally, however, Colum used the opportunity to offer some insight to exegetes into certain seemingly obscure passages of Joyce's work, especially *Finnegans Wake.*

The book is divided into two sections. "Dublin" is ninety-two pages long of which Molly contributed five. She did not know Joyce in Dublin. Although he attended the same university as she did, University College, he was several years ahead of her and although she saw him around, she knew of him only by reputation. Molly quotes a friend: "There is James Joyce, the great genius of University College in his own estimation"(*JJ*, 13). In fact, here and elsewhere, Molly is somewhat self-serving. She identifies herself with Joyce through her "superior" education:

> Joyce and I both matriculated at what was then called the Royal University. It was the successor to the university Cardinal Newman projected, but was nonsectarian—not a Catholic university, that is, though one of its colleges, University College, which Joyce attended, was Catholic. Later the Royal University became the National University. Joyce had his degree from the Royal; I, coming after him, had mine from the National University.
>
> I have often heard the Royal University spoken of disparagingly on the ground that it was not residential, as Dublin University (Trinity College) is. Actually the Royal turned out some of the best educated people I have ever known. It did not give a practical or pragmatic education, but it succeeded in producing cultivated and even learned persons, of whom Joyce was one. (*JJ*, 15–16)

On the other hand, Padraic, in "Dublin," wonderfully evokes the city at the turn of the century, with the eccentric and charismatic figure of the impoverished Joyce shuttling in and out of the narrative's rich fabric. In perhaps the most interesting and significant part of the book Padraic poignantly describes Joyce's great frustration in attempting to get the writer-publisher, George Roberts of Maunsel and Company, to honor his contract for the publication of *Dubliners* (*JJ*, 81–100). Roberts grew frightened of the possibility of libel suits and censorship. He reneged on publication and humiliated Joyce. Colum, an old friend of Roberts, tried to mediate but to no avail. Joyce returned to Trieste and the teaching of English, full of frustra-

tion and anger at the publisher and his native land, both unrecogniz-
ing of his genius. Colum offers a fascinating conjecture:

> Suppose it had been otherwise? Suppose that when he came back to Dub-
> lin this time Joyce had walked into the publishers' office and been handed
> the proofs of his first book? Suppose he had gone back to Trieste with a
> small check on a Dublin bank and a dozen copies of *Dubliners* in his trunk?
> What a different impression he would have had of his native city! Joyce
> would have been happier, of course; his mind would have been free of the
> suspicion of persecution he was prone to. But would there then have been
> a literature of exile? (*JJ*, 86)

"Paris," the second section of *Our Friend James Joyce* contains 230
pages of which forty-six are Molly's. The Colums met Joyce as a couple for the first time in Paris in 1923. It was eleven years since
Colum and Joyce had last met in Dublin. The Colum-Joyce relationship would be as two families from 1923 on. Early in the "Paris"
section Molly attempts to show that she had predicted Joyce's
greatness:

> My husband and I returned to Ireland in 1921, the year *Ulysses* came out.
> I was asked to review the book for the American magazine *The Freeman*, then
> edited by Albert Joy Nock. . . . The opening sentence was a harmless
> enough remark to the effect that within the next couple of decades many
> books would be published on Joyce and *Ulysses*. Nock wrote me an annoyed
> letter saying he was deleting these lines, as they would have been an exag-
> geration if applied to Cervantes or Tolstoi on the publication of any of their
> works. But later he was fond of quoting publicly a version of that sentence,
> and of saying how right I had been. (*JJ*, 111)

Generally, however, Molly is more interested in discussing her relationship with the Joyce children, particularly their daughter Lucia,
who suffered from recurring mental illness and whom Molly tried to
help. Molly is hard on Joyce; she faults him as a father; she is angry
over how he spends money from patrons on excellent food, fine wines,
and generous tips, while her husband has to earn their living by publishing. One gets an impression also, that despite her efforts to appear as a close friend of Joyce, the novelist did not like her very much
and perhaps only put up with her because of his fondness for the easy-
going Padraic, a man always generous with his time and ear. One
berating of Joyce is particularly severe:

Joyce had an odd capacity for acquiring money and patrons, and I can never imagine him as poor as many writers I have known. . . . To Joyce this seemed normal: he was engaged in writing what he, as well as many others, believed to be great works of literature, and he thought it fitting that he should be supported while doing this by those who had the wherewithal to endow him. I know there are many stories told about his poverty, about his having to wear a long-tailed coat to hide the patches on his trousers when he was working in a bank in Rome. These stories are true, I am sure. Still one cannot overlook his extravagance and the extravagance of his family. . . .

Joyce always behaved as though the money he had been given would last forever. I remember one festive dinner he invited us to at Les Frianons, when Nora was away somewhere. Everyone drank a great deal of champagne, and Joyce, departing in an expansive mood, presented each one of a row of bowing waiters—none of whom had been assigned to his table—with a hundred-franc note. I managed, with the help of the proprietor or the head waiter, to collect these hundred-franc notes, giving each waiter ten francs instead. He took Joyce home and put him to bed, and I left the hundred-franc bills I had retrieved in an envelope where he would find them the next morning.

Miss Weaver once wrote Joyce that she knew he was spending money like a drunken sailor. It was after she told him this that Joyce said to my husband, who had no money except what he made by writing, "Morally, you are in a better position than I am." (*JJ*, 189–91)

Padraic Colum, however, delights in the entertaining anecdote that provides insight into his old friend's sensitive, pixyish character. Additionally, Colum, proud that he was asked to write the first introduction to the publication of *Anna Livia Plurabelle* (1928), a part of *Finnegans Wake,* delights in *explication de texte* of small bits of that monumental work. It is as if the poet, having been close to Joyce during some of the time the novelist was writing *Finnegans Wake,* felt a kind of proprietorship toward the book. In fact, he includes most of his original introduction to *Anna Livia Plurabelle* in *Our Friend James Joyce* and he serves as an informal *Notes and Queries* to *Finnegans Wake* (*JJ*, 139–43).

What a good friend Colum was to Joyce. As the novelist's eyesight failed, the poet, although struggling to earn a living for Molly and himself by writing, nevertheless typed portions of the extremely difficult manuscript of *Finnegans Wake.* He, and Molly, too, were always available to help the Joyce children and grandchild, to write letters supporting Joyce's pet causes, to encourage review of Joyce's work in print, to obtain advances from publishers, to raise money for Joyce, and, after Joyce's death in 1941, to help his widow survive. The Padraic Colum part of *Our Friend James Joyce* contains some first-rate storytelling. Colum had the right idea. He left the book light and amusing. The incidents of Joyce's difficult life were heavy enough. As a result, *Our Friend James Joyce* is an excellent supplement, an on-the-spot close-up account of James Joyce, the youth in Dublin and the literary lion of Paris between the wars.

In 1939 the Colums and the Joyces said goodbye, unbeknownst to themselves for the last time, as war clouds loomed on the European horizon. Colum poignantly describes the farewell scene:

> We were obliged soon afterward to leave Paris for New York. Joyce, in spite of many troubles, was on the last pages of what would be entitled *Finnegans Wake*. His good friends and helpers were around him as always, but no one could avoid feeling the anxiety of the time.
>
> We had boarded the boat train when, looking out of the window, we saw Joyce and Nora coming along the platform. They had come to see us off. For ten minutes the four of us were together. We talked to them about being back in a year, about remembrances to friends, about the reception that would be accorded the long-worked-on book. I knew all the time we were talking that for Joyce this was a real separation. In Europe a feeling of desperation was rising; our friends had a personal problem as well, and one of them was learning that it was insoluble. We were going from a continent filled with misgivings and dangers to a continent where violence and stupidity were not threatening the people, and Joyce said this in his well-wishing, it made his well-wishing the more earnest. He was sad, he was lonely, he was resigned; he was here out of an old friendship. It was a very different leave-taking from others we had had from him in the earlier Paris years, when he was the genial Dublin man, happy with family and friends.
>
> "Good-by, Joyce! Luck to *Finnegans Wake*," we called. (*JJ*, 234–35)

The train moved out and a long friendship had come to an end as all must.

Perhaps the words that best describe *Our Friend James Joyce* are illuminating and charming. The biography is illuminating in that it succeeds in presenting Joyce in a most human light. The reader really sees and understands James Joyce, the bachelor youth in Dublin and the middle-aged family man in Paris, far more cogently than he might in a heavier, scholarly biography. It is charming perhaps because it tells the reader almost as much about the Colums as it does about the Joyces. Life in the English-speaking literary circle of Paris during the 1920s and 1930s has seldom been better presented. *Ourselves Alone: The Story of Arthur Griffith and the Origin of the Irish Free State* (1959) is about as different from *Our Friend James Joyce* as two biographies can be. Yet both are about personal friends of Padraic Colum. Rather than a series of reminiscences, *Ourselves Alone* is an exhaustingly thorough, scholarly work on which Colum worked for more than ten years. The Joyce book is about a great literary figure, the kind of person Colum knew and understood well. *Ourselves Alone* studies a politician who became a statesman, a human type with whom Colum had less familiarity.

Colum was not really a trained researcher. Fortunately, Sean Milroy, in the 1940s, worked on a life of Griffith which he could not complete prior to his death. In the preface Colum relates how he came to undertake the project:

ARTHUR GRIFFITH always had a circle of devoted friends, and it was a matter of course that they should try to establish a record of his career; the Irish public, they recognized, had a right to participate through biography in the heroic life of the founder of the Irish state. Soon after his death a representative of his associated friends, Desmond Fitzgerald, approached me as one who had known him with the suggestion I should write his Life. I was unable to undertake the work at the time.

His friends then turned to one who, in later years, had close association with Arthur Griffith, Mr. Sean Milroy. . . .

He died before completing the narrative or bringing the manuscript beyond the first draft. It is mainly factual, containing long extracts from articles written by Arthur Griffith (occasionally by others) dealing with important national topics of the day, and, as a narrative, centering on Griffith the publicist.

After Mr. Milroy's death I was approached again by representatives of Arthur Griffith's friends, most persuasively by Senator Michael Hayes. He placed at my disposal what he and Mr. Desmond Fitzgerald had noted as "the indispensable preliminary materials of any life of Griffith." With this beside him, I recognized that the biographer who undertook to write a complete Life of Arthur Griffith would be spared a quantum of necessary labour, so abundant is it in factual material. This recognition decided me to fall in with the request of the friends of Arthur Griffith. Mr. Milroy's narrative was of inestimable help to me in writing this biography.[7]

Arthur Griffith (1871–1922) was a leader of the passive resistance part of the Irish Revolution. Straight out of an English jail, he be-

came the first president of the newly established Irish Free State in
1922, and he died suddenly and unexpectedly in August of that same
year as a shocking civil war developed. When a young man he worked
as a printer and later he became the editor of the influential revolutionary periodical, the *United Irishman*. It was as a contributor to that
publication that Colum met Griffith and they became lifelong
friends. Colum was deeply shocked by Griffith's death. He considered
his friend to be a martyr to Irish freedom.

Ourselves Alone is more than a biography. Colum chose to use the
life of Arthur Griffith as an architectonic for presenting the history of
the political and cultural development that led to Irish independence
and that produced a great flowering of Irish culture unparalleled since
the Middle Ages. Colum documents the fight for freedom from the
birth of the Sinn Fein party through the controversial acceptance of
the treaty with Britain and the establishment of the Irish Free State
in 1922.

Clearly, Colum had a wide audience in mind for *Ourselves Alone*.
He was not merely writing for his contemporaries, many of whom
had lived through the experiences he shared and depicted. He was
now writing for the American audience, for the English audience who
needed to see the Griffith side of the issues, and, most important, for
the generations of Irish yet to come.

The book's weakness lies in the fact that Colum was not very much
at home with research and with scholarly writing. The writing is
stilted and obtuse. The reader could wish that Colum had chosen a
more informal style, somewhat more like his approach in *Our Friend
James Joyce,* for although one sees the panorama of history quite well
in *Ourselves Alone,* one often loses sight of the nature and the qualities
of Colum's ostensible subject, Arthur Griffith. Occasionally, however, the author's writing skill and his dramatic sensibility turn out
exciting prose, especially when he can bring into his scene a theatrical
personality like heroine Maud Gonne.

On the morning of June 28th the National forces came before the Four
Courts and demanded the surrender of those within. . . .

Madame Gonne MacBride's son, Sean, was still a youngster, but he had
gone into the Four Courts. Maud Gonne went there: the prisoners taken
from the Four Courts, she thought, were being badly treated; it would take
nothing away from the Executive to give orders that they be treated more

humanely. In order to get this done she went to the Government Building and asked to see Arthur Griffith.

And so in the middle of a historic drama, a private drama was briefly enacted. Arthur Griffith was presiding at one of the Cabinet meetings that were being held continuously. Going to the door of the Council Room he met that tall woman whose face would always be beautiful and always vivacious, whose tone of voice would always be more memorable than the tone of any other person's voice, the voice that had chanted in *Cathleen-ni-Houlihan*. In the days of his apprenticeship, the evenings of reunions in Clare Street, the buoyant time of the launching of *The United Irishman* and the starting of the National Theatre, she had been for Arthur Griffith the reincarnation of a past that might be restored—a beautiful and heroic past. And whom did she see? That square-built man who was so genial and so resilient, was no longer upstanding, if we go by a sketch that was made of him at the time, but with bent head, a face that was deeply lined, and with something slow-paced in his firmness. They stood at the door of the Council Chamber in a solid Government Building. She made a plea; he gave a curt answer: "We are now a Government; we have to keep order," and went back to the Cabinet meeting. This was the last time Maud Gonne and Arthur Griffith were to meet. (*OA*, 368–70)

Although *Ourselves Alone* was Padraic Colum's last biographical publication, in reality it was almost a lifelong work based on a lifetime participation in, or observation of, twentieth-century Irish history. The work is generous to the memory of Arthur Griffith. Colum always paid his debts to his friends. Arthur Griffith was certainly no exception.

Essays

Although Padraic Colum contributed essays, reviews, and critical articles for over forty years to periodicals in Dublin, Britain, and America such as the *Saturday Review of Literature, Manchester Guardian,* the *Nation, Catholic World, Commonweal, Dublin Magazine,* and *Dial,* samples of his nonfiction shorter prose are more easily located and best experienced in his collections of essays, often culled from the periodicals: *My Irish Year* (1912), *The Road Round Ireland* (1926), *Cross Roads in Ireland* (1930), and *A Half-Day's Ride:* or *Estates in Corsica* (1932).

My Irish Year is a propagandistic collection of political essays and observations, and some stories and poems too, depicting rural life in

southern Ireland. Colum writes from firsthand observations made in
the Midlands and the west of Ireland. He states the geographical and
social limitations of the work in his introduction:

"My Irish Year" is not representative of the whole of Ireland: Catholic and
Peasant Ireland only is shown, and this Catholic and Peasant Ireland is lo-
calised in a strip of country crossing the Midlands to the West. . . . Still,
if not representative of the whole of Ireland, "My Irish Year" is representative of a great part of Ireland. The life described may stand for the life of
the Catholic peasantry. And the Catholic peasantry are not merely the bulk
of the Irish population; they are, roughly speaking, the historic Irish
nation.[8]

Colum has a very keen eye for detail in *My Irish Year,* the eye that
helped him to enrich his novels and stories. In fact, the travel essay
collections were, in part, preparation for his work as a novelist, particularly for the writing of what he hoped would be his fictional epic
of the Irish nation, *The Flying Swans.* His depiction of the Irish country town is typical of his fine descriptive power:

The Irish country town is harsh and ugly, for it has been built by people
who are still in the pastoral stage. The street is wide for the movement of
herds. Four out of every five are public-houses. In the depths of these shops,
one can see bacon and boots, reaping machines, and sacks of lime. . . .
    There is neither fair or market to-day, and the town looks dead. Before
the steps of the Courthouse three or four men are standing in discussion;
their appearance is provincial rather than rural; they are members of the District Council, and they had a meeting to-day. Three or four young men,
who have a certain fierceness of aspect, assemble near. They have ash plants
in their hands, and one might guess that there was a question of awarding
labourers cottages at the meeting to-day. There is a discontented party
within the labour group; it breaks up, and the men part shaking ash plants,
and shouting threats at each other.
    Besides its main street, the town has its bog road. The bog road goes off
at the single arm of a sign-post. It opens to the brown region of the bog,
while the main street leads to the grazing country. In the latter street the
houses are thatched, and some show a cup and saucer in the window as a
sign that refreshment is provided. Here there is the cart-builder's stall. I am
always taken by the round, bright-coloured wheels that are soon to travel on
the road. (*IY,* 9–10)

The essay on the Irish rural economy is informative and historically
correct. It argues well for a political party based on agrarian interests

in order to provide for a better-fed society. His comments on the Irish immigrant in America are accurate and, again, based on personal observations. Colum also deals with religion in popular poetry and the folklore of the area. The author delights in long character sketches such as "Ballad-Singer," "An Agrarian Priest," "The County Schoolmaster," "A Grazier," and "The Country Trader." The Colum reader is reminded of the early powerful poems such as "The Plougher," "A Drover," and "A Poor Scholar of the Forties."

Colum included "The Flute Player's Story" in *My Irish Year*. Later he would include stories first appearing in this book in his later travel essay collections. This republication without citation is a kind of deception he occasionally practiced, as when, also, he repeated descriptions, only changing the place names.[9]

My Irish Year succeeds, however, in doing exactly what he intended. It presents the flavor of the Irish countryside. It leaves the reader with a belief that she has been there and now knows the topography, the culture, and the hopes and dreams of the people of the place.

The Road Round Ireland contains most of *My Irish Year* in parts I and II, "The Midlands" and "Abroad in Breifny," and "Eilis's Story" is slipped in too. The anti-English propaganda is omitted as by 1926 Ireland was independent of Britain. Colum then goes on to write about "Connacht and Donegal" (Part III), "Louth, Meath, and the County Dublin" (Part IV), "Dublin through the Abbey Theatre" (Part V), "Leinster" (Part VI), and "Into Munster" (Part VII).

By far the most interesting section of *The Road Round Ireland* is the discussion of Irish theater history and the various "Dublins": George Moore's, Arthur Griffith's, James Joyce's, Seumas O'Sullivan's, and James Stephens's. Colum's remarks about Joyce will be incorporated in *Our Friend James Joyce*. He offers generous criticism of the playwright who had become the outstanding newer product of the Abbey Theatre, Sean O'Casey:

> To get its most general feature, one should have Dublin presented by a writer who knows intimately the life of the tenement-house, and who has belonged to the world of unskilled and casual labour. The dramatist of "Juno and the Paycock" is such a writer. He was brought up in the tenement-house side of the city where Dublin life is most native—on the north side (born, by the way, a few streets from where Richard Brinsley Sheridan was born). . . . Sean O'Casey has worked at nearly all the casual jobs that fall to the lot of the unskilled, uncollared worker in Dublin: he has been a

dock-labourer, a hod-carrier, a stone-breaker on the roads; as a boy he
worked in Dublin's big news-agency for nine shillings per week; he had to
be on the job at four o'clock in the mornings to get the newspapers folded
and addressed for the early trains, and he was dismissed from his job for not
holding his cap in his hand while his pay was being given him.

All this, however, would be of little avail to him as a dramatist if he did
not also love the men and women, the boys and girls he has known in the
tenements and met on the various jobs he has put his hands to. He loves
them and he believes in them.[10]

Colum recognized that O'Casey had something new and different
to offer the drama. O'Casey was a city dweller and a person intimately acquainted with tenement life, who could bring to the Irish
theater the kind of insight into the Dublin character that Joyce
brought to the novel:

Sean O'Casey has discovered a new material: he has shifted the centre of
dramatic interest from the peasant to the dwellers of the city tenements.
Unlike the other dramatists who departed from the country cottage he discovered a material which is just as rich as the traditional material of the
Abbey play. Dublin has its own folk-life and its own communal tradition,
and he has been the first to put that life and that tradition on the stage.
(RRI, 267)

Colum's description of literary Ireland serves as an excellent introduction to and primer of the pre- and post-independence world of
Irish letters and politics. It shows his ability not only to write about
the Irish countryside but to introduce and explain at an early date
some of the most important books of the twentieth century such as
James Joyce's *Dubliners, Portrait of the Artist as a Young Man,* and
Ulysses.

In "Leinster" Colum also deals with his old, now long-dead Abbey
colleague, John Millington Synge. Over twenty pages of the book are
devoted to Synge and his work. As always, Colum is generous, and
as usual correct in his judgment of his fellow writers:

It might be said of him that at the very start of the Irish Theatre he
brought in a way of looking at life that belongs essentially to the Gaelic
tradition. His plays were denounced as being alien to Irish life and to the
Irish mind. Those who denounced them in these terms were wrong, and
they were wrong because they knew nothing about the Gaelic tradition as it

has been expressed in poetry—in the poetry of the seventeenth and eighteenth centuries. (*RRI*, 370–71)

If for no other reason, *The Road Round Ireland* is worth reading for its fresh, still vibrant commentary on those people and events who made the Irish Renaissance. Colum's light approach and easy manner adds not only to the enjoyment of the book but also to a delightful sense of being there for the reader.

In *Cross Roads in Ireland* Colum revisits some locations dealt with in *My Irish Year* and *The Road Round Ireland,* but most of the book is fresh and much of it discusses Northern Ireland. Again, besides descriptive essays, it includes short stories and political and literary biographies. A discussion of the life of Oliver Goldsmith receives twenty-two pages in "The South," and Colum's favorite military hero, Michael Collins, is well remembered.

He was an extraordinarily energized man. A scholar-friend of mine who saw him at the Griffith funeral said that he radiated power, that one felt that by touching him one would gain in vitality. For over two years there was hardly a day, hardly a night, in which he was not in danger of meeting a violent end. This was when people were becoming aware that in the partially smothered warfare that was being waged with the British power he was the most notable of the champions.[11]

The book ends on a military note. "Shannon Saga: Brian's Battle" tells the story of a defeat of the Norsemen, first related in their *Njal Saga* by King Brian of Ireland in the eleventh century. Colum's stirring account of a battle that took place on land that is part of the City of Dublin, a battle that may be an allegory for the recent ouster of the British, ends with a lament, for the Irish king dies at the very end of the battle and Colum could have been alluding to Arthur Griffith, who died just as the Irish had achieved the Free State and the civil war began. He ends the story and the book with a poem in Anglo-Saxon versification:

> I say that king mighty
> To death now is done,
> Now low before spear-point
> That earl bows his head.
> Soon over all Ersemen
> Sharp sorrow shall fall.
>
> (*CRI*, 374–75)

A Half-Day's Ride; or Estates in Corsica is a collection of twenty-four essays and articles previously published in Colum's usual outlets like the *Saturday Review of Literature* and *Dublin Magazine.* Some are literary pieces, others are travel articles on such diverse places as Paris, Hollywood, Hawaii, and New York. One-fourth of the book deals with Hawaii. *A Half-Day's Ride's* heterogeneousness is the main weakness; although the individual pieces are charming, informative, always interesting, and very well written, the book lacks cohesion. Although Ireland is missing, the Hawaiians seem Irish. Colum points up their close family structure, the poetry in their language, and their ever-present awareness of their history.

The title, *A Half-Day's Ride; or Estates in Corsica,* comes from Colum's reading of and enjoying a little-read novel, *A Day's Ride, A Life's Romance* by Charles Lever. The hero, Colum tells us in his first essay, "A Day's Ride," is a man named Potts, a charlatan, who claims his family had "estates in Corsica." Potts's fabrications remind Colum of the pretender in himself and in us all, and he resolves to read unrecommended books and to travel where no one wants to take him. But then, with a wink, he says, "Here I am imitation Potts, talking as if I expected the public to believe that I own estates in Corsica."[12]

Colum's observation of life in twentieth-century Europe and America had grown very sharp by 1932, and the provincial Irish writer had developed into a most cosmopolitan world citizen, at home in Paris or London as well as in New York and Dublin. A little bit of cynicism crept into his character and his writing, as evidenced by two especially insightful essays in *A Half-Day's Ride,* "Miss Europe" and "A Marine Adventure." In the former Colum has been appointed a judge for the Miss Europe contest and he has a chance to see a group of very beautiful women, including their legs:

Miss Espagne seemed to say, "Here are my legs; there's nothing wrong with them." Miss France showed her garters as well as her knees. (*HDR,* 18)

Of course, as an inveterate classicist, Colum immediately adores Miss Greece:

Imagine a dark-skinned and very slender girl sheathed in silver: the features were like those on a medallion, her hair in a knot on her neck. When I say "dark-skinned" I am, perhaps, too emphatic: I suppose her skin was really olive. When she stood upon the platform and raised her arms, or held back her head, or turned a hand, she took, naturally and simply, the lines of a tanagra or painting on a vase. Dividing her long silver skirt she showed her legs to the knees. She did this so charmingly that I, for one, felt like applauding as one applauds when one sees a surprisingly graceful gesture in the ballet. She seemed to say to us "In the Peloponnesus there is still a remnant of the Hellenic race. I happen to be that survival. I am sure, messieurs, you are delighted to come so close to the most aristocratic type that Europe has produced." (*HDR*, 18–19)

In the end, however, Colum is disappointed with her too. His beautiful symbol of ancient Greece is "too much at home in this world." The lovely statue is "not Hellenic but Byzantine; not Nausicaa nor Helen, but Theodora or Theophano. Europe had gone back to Byzance" (*HDR*, 20).

"A Marine Adventure" is another article about modern women and their sexual appeal to a writer who cannot help but see them in symbolic and historical contexts. When visiting an aquarium in the Bahamas filled with exotic and fierce fish, he sees a beautiful if vacuous girl serving as a guide. She seems to him to be a siren by the sea and his description of their encounter shows his love for the beauty of women, his acceptance of their power over men, his disappointment that beauty sometimes is not accompanied by intellect or knowledge, and his middle-age pique over being rejected by a pretty, young girl. The writing is shaved to the bone: sparse, cutting, without waste:

"Any information you'd like to have?" The young lady in charge of the watery exhibition spoke to me. She was closed in with pieces of coral and by those fan-shaped growths that may be coral or hardened sponges, by huge round sponges and great shells that had in them the colors of dawns and sunsets. She had been powdering her nose, or putting stick on her lips, or combing her hair since my entrance. . . . "Aren't you changing the color of your lips?" I said.

"To geranium," said she. "I spend most of my time making up."

"It would be nice to see you outside," I ventured. "There is dancing on the beach. . . ."

"Oh, I never can dance," she cried, and the corals and sponges and shells did not permit my seeing her feet. "And I never keep appointments," she said.

"Of course not," I agreed. "And I am very lucky to be able to come on you here and have you talk to me."

"Any information I can give you?" she began.

"What songs the Sirens sang . . ." I murmured.
"What about them?" she said.
"None of us know what they were," I said. "You can tell me."
"No one ever asks me about them," she said.
"It has long been thought," I went on, "that they are not beyond all con-
jecture. But I want very much to hear what they were."
"Don't you know?" she asked.
"No. Tell me. The songs the Sirens sang—what were they?"
"They were the usual songs," she replied. (*HDR*, 93–94)

Colum's four essay collections show the author as a personable, humorous, relaxed writer, competent in his informal style. From the
first three he extracted the concept of the itinerant structure of *Poet's
Circuits*. Colum himself is very much a subject of these books and the
reader comes to know the author better in these works than in any
other of his writings with the possible exceptions of *Our Friend James
Joyce* and *Images of Departure*.

The prose of Padraic Colum serves to prove his overall and general
ability as a writer. Although his poetry and early plays are his major
contribution to literature, Colum's novels, biographies, and essays
can only add to his reputation in the long run.

Chapter Seven
A Gift for the Young: Folklore, Mythology, and Books for Children

For over forty years of his life Padraic Colum published books for children, books for young adults, and popular folklore and mythology. He was a storyteller, not a trained folklorist. He was a translator of cultural histories: European, ancient Greek, Hawaiian, and especially Irish, for the younger generation of any time. He began to learn the storyteller's craft as a child in Ireland sitting by the fire and listening to adults, especially Micky Burns and the people of the workhouse. He learned folklore as an avid reader in libraries all over the world. The twenty-five or more volumes of his storytelling for the young, and those interested in the mythological past, represent the bulk of Colum's prose, and the means by which he earned of his livelihood for half of his lifetime. The work for the young and the study of folklore are all of one piece because they are all part of a single purpose: passing on the moral values of the past to future generations.

Colum's storytelling is always purposeful, gentle, humble, humorous, simple, and careful not to shock, disturb, or offend youthful sensitivity and idealism. Although this work is not as important, critically speaking, as his poetry, his dramas, or perhaps even his two novels, still it is no small contribution, and judging by the fact that several of his children's books are still in print, the gift to Ireland of his lyric poetry may be in time nearly matched by his gift to the young of myth, history, and the art of the simple story well told. In spirit his writing for children is closer to his poetry and his drama than to his fictional, critical, or biographical prose in that he struggles for terseness, lucidity, and dramatic impact.

Although Colum's successful career as a writer of books for youth really began in New York when he joined with the popular illustra-

tor, Willy Pogány, in presenting *The King of Ireland's Son* (1916), his
first book for youth, *A Boy in Eirinn* (1913), was in part written in
Ireland, although penned for Americans. Colum was cutting his eye
teeth in this work because the book is clearly a crass, heavy-handed,
propaganda piece designed to invoke American sympathy for the
cause of Irish independence. Supposedly, *A Boy in Eirinn* depicts the
life of a typical Irish lad. Finn O'Donnell's father is languishing in an
English jail because of his organizing work with oppressed Irish farmers, while Finn's mother is in America working to support the family. Finn lives with his grandparents, and he observes Irish history in
the making.

As a novel for children, *A Boy in Eirinn* has a few successes. First,
the description of both the Irish countryside and the City of Dublin
are excellent. Secondly, the child reader has no trouble in feeling a
part of the book's milieu and identifying with the children in the
story. Colum's patriotism surely seemed strident after the establishment of the Irish Free State, yet *A Boy in Eirinn* went through five
editions in America and in England.

One particularly interesting aspect of Colum's first book for children is that Colum has Finn watch a one-act, four-scene Irish play,
which Colum includes in its entirety. The play is a dramatization of
the saga, "The Destruction of Da Derga's Hostel," a tale of ancient
Ireland.

In 1929 Colum updated the book to show Finn's life as an adult,
contributing to the growth and development of free, industrialized
Ireland.

In *The King of Ireland's Son* (1916) Colum passed on the stories he
had learned in his grandmother's house. The book caused him to be
labeled a folklorist and mythologist and he went with it.[1] Colum's
humor abounds in this informally structured work of Irish folklore
and legend. His animals are funny, vain, vulnerable "humans." He
talks to his young readers as a peer, conspiring against literal-
minded, incredulous adults. The two narratives, that of the Prince
and of Prince Flann who turns out to be a brother, complement each
other well. The King of Ireland's son quests for his lady love, Fed-
elma, and Flann quests for his personal identity. On the architectonic
of the plots hang delicious animal fables, poems, political and religious allegories, fairy tales, and mock epics. In the end all turns out
well, as all quests succeed. The younger readers of Colum's book receive a large dose of Irish culture steeped in the melted sugar of fan-

ciful storytelling, while enjoying the simple, satisfying plots. The vocabulary and the style are appropriate to youth but not condescending. Colum would never write down to his younger readers.

The Boy Who Knew What the Birds Said (1918) is a wonderful miracle tale for grade-schoolers about a boy who prevents the world from coming to an end and is rewarded by the gift of understanding the language of the birds. The boy's saving deed is to stop "The Bird that Follows the Cuckoo" from flying into the cuckoo's mouth, which would cause the world to end. Colum's premise is outrageous enough to enthrall even the most jaded child reader or listener. All the subsequent stories in the book, including "The Stone of Victory," feature such birds as grouse, wrens, plovers, eagles, woodpeckers, falcons, chickens, peewits, blackbirds, starlings, finches, linnets, swans, ravens, crows, pigeons, doves, kingfishers, and peacocks. Here, as elsewhere in his work, Colum pays loving homage to the beasts of the air. Of course, *The Boy Who Knew What the Birds Said* has the usual share of adventures and quests complete with brave youths, beautiful princesses, mighty kings, and evil giants.

The Adventures of Odysseus (1918) is part of Colum's world epic collection. In it he closely follows Homer's *Odyssey*. The major variations are simplification of character and a slight reduction of violence. However, the quality of the prose is high and an adult reader clearly would enjoy the book too. It ends with a storytelling flare:

> So ends the story of Odysseus who went with King Agamemnon to the wars of Troy; who made the plan of the Wooden Horse by which Priam's City was taken at last; who missed the way of his return, and came to the Land of the Lotus-eaters; who came to the Country of the dread Cyclopes, to the Island of AEolus and to the house of Circe, the Enchantress; who heard the song of the Sirens, and came to the Rocks Wandering, and to the terrible Charybdis, and to Scylla, past whom no other man had won scatheless; who landed on the Island where the Cattle of the Sun grazed, and who stayed upon Ogygia, the home of the nymph Calypso; so ends the story of Odysseus, who would have been made deathless and ageless by Calypso if he had not yearned always to come back to his own hearth and his own land. And in spite of all his troubles and his toils he was fortunate, for he found a constant wife and a dutiful son and a father still alive to weep over him.[2]

The Girl Who Sat by the Ashes (1919) is Colum's version of the Cinderella story. In it the wicked stepmother works for the prince as supervisor of not one but three balls as the prince tries to find the proper woman for his wife. Colum presents the prince as something of an upper-class English prig, arrogant and supercilious, who needs and gets a taking down. The changes to the oversized fairy tale add fun and zest and surprise to *The Girl Who Sat By the Ashes*.

"Cinderella's" name in *The Girl Who Sat by the Ashes* is Maid-alone. At least that is what she calls herself. Others call her Girl-go-with-the-Goats. Colum's hyphenated names are always a linguistic, imagistic delight. The prince's name for her is "matchless maiden." The magic glass slipper is a golden shoe. The castle has been her place of employment. In the end she returns to rule it with her husband, but not in triumph. Instead she will never forget her humble origins and the good fortune that led her to happiness.

The Boy Apprenticed to an Enchanter (1920) is the fantasy story of Eean, a fisherman's son who defeats the evil Babylonian enchanter, Zabulum, with the help of the horses of King Manus, ruler of the Western Island, and also with the aid of a lovely girl named Bird-of-Gold, who is the bramble-gatherer's daughter. Merlin the Magician also participates in the long, skillful, enchanting narrative.

This British enchanter, at the age of forty, falls in love with a vivacious and beautiful fifteen-year-old, Vivien, who cons him out of his chief charm and enchants him. She is jealous:

When she came back, and when she met him in the hidden garden; she caught hold of his hands, and she would not let go of them. Nor would she tell Merlin why this change had come over her, and why she would keep close to him now and not apart. At last she said to him, "What ladies and what maidens have you known, O my master Merlin?"

Then Merlin took his Magic Glass into his hands, and in it he showed her all the ladies who were at the court of the King of the Isle of Britain, and he showed her all the lovely maidens who lived in far countries and in distant castles whom he knew. Vivien threw herself on the ground with her face to the rock after she had looked into the Magic Glass.[3]

In the end, however, Merlin and Vivien sail off together in happiness and for life, never to be seen again.

Colum uses the quest motif yet again, but in linking together Europe and the Middle East he takes such imaginative leaps that *The Boy Apprenticed to an Enchanter* has some of the strength and power of a great medieval romance like *Sir Gawain and the Green Knight*.

The Children of Odin (1920), a book of Norse myths, is a part of his work on the epics of the world. The book is divided into four sections: Part I, "The Dwellers in Asgard," the stories of the Gods and the Giants; Part II, "Odin the Wanderer"; Part III, "The Witch's Heart" in which Colum treats the evil doings of Loki and his punishment, as well as the legend of the Valkyrie; Part IV, "The Sword of the Volsungs and the Twilight of the Gods." This section is the strongest in the book partly because Colum realized, as did Richard Wagner, that the epic romances of Sigmund and Sigurd were the stuff of tragedy. The description of Sigurd's and Brynhild's funeral is visually powerful:

> They bore Sigurd out of the Hall and Brynhild went beside where they placed him. She took a sword and put it through her own heart. Thus died Brynhild who had been made a mortal woman for her disobedience to the will of Odin, and who was won to be a mortal's wife by a falseness.
> They took Sigurd and his horse Grani, and his helmet and his golden war-gear and they left all on a great painted ship. They could not but leave Brynhild beside him, Brynhild with her wondrous hair and her stern and beautiful face. They left the two together and launched the ship on the sea. And when the ship was on the water they fired it, and Brynhild once again lay in the flames.
> And so Sigurd and Brynhild went together to join Baldur and Nanna in Hela's habitation.[4]

Everywhere in this excellent work on mythology Colum's prose is direct, clear, and strong. The language indeed is as stark as the legend:

SIGURD went to war: with the men that King Alv gave him he marched into the country that was ruled over by the slayer of his father. The war that he waged was short and the battles that he won were not perilous. Old was King Lygni now, and feeble was his grasp upon his people. Sigurd slew him and took away his treasure and added his lands to the lands of King Alv. (*CO*, 215)

The Golden Fleece and the Heroes Who Lived before Achilles (1921) is another one of Colum's world epics. Like *The Adventures of Odysseus* and *The Children of Odin*, this book went through many editions up to and through the 1960s. They remain widely read and enjoyed by children. The sparse accounting of Jason and his Argonauts' quest for

the golden fleece is fleshed out by Colum's inventions and adaptations
of other adventures of the heroes who served as crew of the *Argo,*
among them Heracles, Orpheus, Tiphys, and Nauklis. The building
of the *Argo,* the long voyage to Colchis, the story of Medea, the return to Greece, and the burning of the great ship are all told with
conciseness, clarity, and power. By the time Colum wrote *The Golden
Fleece* he had developed a superb style for young readers and he obtained a following of adults, teachers, and librarians, who realized
that the poet consistently provided books and stories of high literary
quality, often based on the best of world literary classics. They de-
pended on his storytelling abilities, his knowledge of world culture,
his careful work, and his good taste. They were never disappointed.

The *Children Who Followed the Piper* (1922) is Colum's version of the
Pied Piper of Hamlin story. In Colum's story the children are older,
some have reached puberty, and a boy and girl fall in love. Colum's
love narrative centers on the adventures and quests of three of the
children after they are led from Hamlin by the piper, a boy-piper
who is the god Mercury. Thus the book is an amalgamation of fairy
tale and mythology. The god Mars and the sorcerer Circe also appear.

The three protagonists are the milk woman's child, Golden Hood;
the miller's son, John Ball; and the emperor's son, Valentine. Golden
Hood and Valentine marry. John Ball grows jealous and is turned to
stone for his transgressions. A child's magic touch restores the friend
to life and all live happily ever after. In *The Children Who Followed the
Piper* Colum merely uses the Hamlin story as a launching site for a
tale of knightly questing and adventure.

The *Island of the Mighty, Being the Hero Stories of Celtic Britain Re-
Told* (1924) is a collection of British Celtic stories and a part of
Colum's world epics series. It was not as successful as the others and
did not come out in many subsequent editions as they did. The book
is based on the legends of heroes first told in the ancient Welsh collection of heroic tales, *The Mabinogion.* However, the book is more of
an editing job by Colum than an original work. The prose is primarily the 1838 effort of Lady Charlotte Guest and the book sorely lacks
Colum's style and humor. His introduction, nevertheless, is a fine ex-
planation of the significance of *The Mabinogion.* He has studied early
Celtic history and is acutely aware of the joint Welsh (Cymric), Scottish, Cornish, and Irish history. He finds the medieval Welsh guild
of bards with its apprenticeship system of training young storytellers

to be the main reason for the survival of the *Arthuriad* and much of the cultural inheritance of the Gaels.

Other significant editing by Colum of children's books includes *Gulliver's Travels* (1919) and *The Arabian Nights* (1953). The former went through two popular editions.

The Peep-Show Man (1924) is a work for very young children, a sixty-five-page book with only three stories in it, the first of which is that of the Peep-Show Man himself, who carries his show in a black box on his back. His is a story for Midsummer Day and is called "The Princess Swallow-Heart." It is about the winning of the princess by her swain. "The Twelve Silly Sisters That the Pooka Carried Away with Him" is a mystery story for Halloween. Lastly, "The White Blackbird," a story for Easter, is about a lonely boy who captures a white blackbird, which, through love, helps him to a reconciliation with his soldier father. This last story is one of Colum's most moving short, short stories for children.

Six Who Were Left in a Shoe (1924) was first published in London by Brentano in a limited, boxed edition and not made available for American readers. In 1968, however, McGraw-Hill brought out an edition of this book for young children. It is the story of the Old Woman Who Lived in a Shoe revisited after her children had gone. Because she had the "best broomstick in the country . . . the fairies [take] her off to brush the cobwebs off . . . the sky."[5] Left behind in the shoe are a dog, a cat, a goat, a goose, a little speckled hen, a pigeon, and a wren. Missing the Old Woman, and not knowing what to do, they set out on a journey, with the goat as leader, to find a new home.

Colum's two books on Hawaiian folklore, *At The Gateways of the Day* (1924) and *The Bright Islands* (1925), later brought out in a single revised volume as *Legends of Hawaii* (1937), represent his most carefully researched work in this genre. He studied the Hawaiian language. He did research out in the field. He carefully compared the myths and legends of Hawaii with European myths and legends in order to understand better the universality of mythic experience.[6] Yale University Press published the books for the Hawaiian Legend and Folklore Commission. Most important, Colum worked diligently for the children of Hawaii, those he met and those who would come to his book in future generations to learn of their cultural past in the only surviving way (*AGD*), xvii).

Much of Colum's material came from the Fornander Collection of Hawaiian Antiquities and Folklore, first gathered in the early part of the nineteenth century. *At the Gateways of the Day* contains the great myths and legends of the Polynesian peoples presented with style and content appropriate to younger readers. Beginning with a section on "Kings of the Islands," *The Bright Islands* contains more historical material. Together these books are to this day the seminal work on Hawaiian folklore.

Typical of both story line and prose style in *At the Gateways of the Day* is the opening of "The Story of Ha-le-ma-no and the Princess Kama":

In Puna lived the Princess Kama, and she was so beautiful that two Kings strove to win her—the King of Puna and the King of Hilo. They sent presents to her mother and to her father and to herself. But Kama never saw either of those Kings. She was sent to live in a house that no one was permitted to enter except herself and her brother. "In a while Kama will come to the height of her beauty," her parents said, "and then we will give her to be Queen to one of these Kings. But until that time comes no one must speak to her." And so, in a house that was forbidden to every one else, Kama lived with only her young brother for her companion. (*AGD*, 93)

The legend gets down to business immediately with no nonsense. It contains a beautiful princess, desired by kings, and a young lover pining away for her. A Western reader, however, cannot help but notice that the charming story could have been, save for the exotic names, a medieval romance or a Renaissance English ballad like "Barbara Allen."

The Bright Islands works much the same way. In the "Kings of the Islands" section the reader is introduced to Umi the Conquerer, just as Colum might introduce "The King of Ireland's Son."

UMI was the son of Liloa, the King. But Umi was born far from the King's house, and his mother was not of rank equal to the King's. And so Umi was reared up just as a country boy.

After he was born his mother married a countryman. But she brought up her son carefully, and he grew to be a sturdy boy. He played all the games that were known at the time, and wherever he went a crowd of boys went with him. When they would come in from playing Umi would give his comrades all the food there was in the house.[7]

Ultimately, the appeal of Colum's Hawaiian work to English-speaking readers lies in the above illustration. It is that his simple, direct, graceful prose underlines the universality of archetypal experiences such as love, lust, greed, generosity, kindness, and the quest for beauty. It is because the legends of Hawaii, except for names and places, are the legends of all the human race.

The Forge in the Forest (1925) is a collection of eight stories, two each about the four elements of the ancient world: earth, air, fire, and water. The themes of the stories are biblical, folk, and Greek. A king takes pleasure in working a forge. As he begins to shape a horseshoe and places it in the fire he calls for stories about the elements from four brothers. The collection ends with a poem praising the craft of the blacksmith. Colum clearly implies that the storyteller is a smith who creates items of beauty and usefulness out of the basic elements. The book is magnificently illustrated by Boris Artzybasheff.

The Voyagers, Being Legends and Romances of Atlantic Discovery (1925) is another one of Colum's world epics and, like the others, is written for children only in that it emphasizes simple syntax and sentence construction. The book incorporates surviving firsthand accounts of explorations of the New World. Colum begins with the legend of Atlantis and such voyages as that of Maeldiun and the Irish sailor-monk Saint Brendan, through the Vikings' adventures in North America, to the coming of Columbus and the Spaniards. Colum provides the storytelling structure for the book by having a wise old Greek from Byzantium and other scholars visit the astronomical tower of Prince Henry the Navigator of Portugal, where they relate to Prince Henry's captains the legends of exploration before their time. The format works well. Columbus's father-in-law-to-be is in the audience and so Colum is able to extend the architectonic to the later, historically documented voyages. Not surprisingly, except for the explorations of Columbus, the Irish tales of the voyage of Maeldiun and the voyage of Saint Brendan in his hide and wickerware vessel receive the bulk of attention. *The Voyagers* is truly a book to stimulate a young adolescent's imagination, and although, perhaps because of its imbalance, it did not go through several reprintings and re-issues, it remains one of Colum's finer efforts in children's literature.

The Fountain of Youth. Stories to be Told (1927) is a collection of stories all of which had been published elsewhere in such diverse books

as *A Boy in Eirinn* and *At the Gateways of the Day*. It also contains the
first version of the essay, "Storytelling, New and Old," about which
more will be said later.

Orpheus. Myths of the World (1930) is the last of Colum's world epics. Although many of the stories in *Orpheus* were published previously, Colum claimed that the book was written as a reference work
for students of mythology.[8] In a long preface he discusses the significance of mythology and introduces the cultures he draws upon for
his collection: Egyptian, Babylonian, Persian, Jewish, Greek, Roman, Graeco-Roman, Celtic, Finnish, Iceland, Indian, Chinese, Japanese, Polynesian, Peruvian, Central American and Mexican, and
Zuñi. The book is tightly organized, beautifully illustrated by Boris
Artzybasheff, and indexed. Because of its preface, organization, and
indexing it is an important addition to the research literature of folklore and mythology. Somewhat comparable in effect to *The Poet's Circuits*, the fifty-nine stories are Colum's most scholarly and significant
statement in the field even though each is written in a language and
style appropriate to young readers. Colum explains why he called this
collection of world folklore *Orpheus*:

I have called the collection "Orpheus," naming it after the minstrel who,
according to the poet of the Argonautica, sang "how the earth, the heaven,
and the sea once mingled together in one form, after deadly strife were sep-
arated each from the other; and how the stars and the moon and the paths
of the sun ever keep their fixed place in the sky; and how the mountains
rose, and how the resounding rivers with their nymphs came into being,
and all creeping things."[9]

The Big Tree of Bunlahy. Stories of My Own Countryside (1933), like
the *King of Ireland's Son*, is a book on Irish subjects, but unlike the
latter or *The Legend of Saint Columba* and *The Frenzied Prince*, it is not
a collection of myths, but is rather a free-wheeling group of stories
directly from Colum's fertile imagination. The narratives are both
melodramatic and humorous. *The Big Tree of Bunlahy*, although a
children's book, nevertheless, captures much of the impact and spirit
of an adult prose work like *The Road Round Ireland* (1926). The title
story is about a great old tree under which people sit and share stories. Twelve other narratives treat various denizens of an Irish town,
such as a shoemaker's daughter, a lawyer's clerk, a cobbler, a black-

smith, a scholar, and a priest. The young reader receives a wonderfully magic sense of place from the book, which is illustrated by the fine painter, Jack Yeats, brother of William Butler Yeats. Another kind of "illustration" in the book is Colum's use of short verse to punctuate high points in the story. *The Big Tree of Bunlahy* seems destined to remain a minor classic of Anglo-Irish children's literature.

The White Sparrow (1933), like *The Peep-Show Man,* is a book to be read to preschool children. It is an allegory about the difficulty and the value of differentness. Jimmie, the white sparrow, undergoes many adventures in the bird world, the land animal world, and the human world. In the last-mentioned he is snared and his flight feathers are clipped. Fortunately, he cleverly escapes in a pelican's beak and eventually returns home to the heart of Paris, where he lives happily ever after with his lady-love sparrow, and where they raise their chicks.

The White Sparrow is a delightful tale. Colum is at his sweetest and gentlest, and clearly enjoying the writing of the book. Jimmie's sadness at the realization that he is different is indicative of the style and sensitivity of the book:

And then he saw his own breast and saw it was different—white. He fluttered his wings and, looking at them, saw that they were white except for their very ends. He was odd—he knew that now. He wished he hadn't come upon the lawn where everybody looked at him. He wished he could go back to his nest and stay there. He crouched upon the grass and made a cry like a very young bird. No one came to him, and he felt so downhearted that he wouldn't have cared if the sky fell down on him.[10]

The Legend of Saint Columba (1935) is another of Colum's Irish books of legends and tales for children. More unified than the other three, it is basically a narrative of Saint Columba's life and trials although some other stories are woven into the fabric of the book. St. Columba (521–597 A.D.), although presented as both a religious and a nationalistic figure, is, nevertheless, cast in a human mold with weaknesses as well as strengths. *The Legend of Saint Columba* is Colum's most serious book for children. The author expresses his deep reverence for the Roman Catholic religion. Also, by treating Saint Columba as an early Irish hero, Colum is able to transmit his

great respect for the history of his native country to his young readers. The book ends with a long, adult, and very patriotic note in
which Colum extols the Celtic contribution to Western culture during the Middle Ages. He also explains the sources of his information
on Saint Columba.

Where the Winds Never Blew and the Cocks Never Crew (1940) is, like
The White Sparrow, a story to be read to preschool children. The setting this time is not an exotic city like the City of Paris in *The White
Sparrow,* but rather a simple farmyard. The adventure of domestic animals provides opportunity for Colum to insert moral values into his
narrative. At the end the animals die. They cross "the edge of the
world" to the place "where they never see their shadows."[11] While
they live, a good old woman cares for them. In the end a cricket who
sings like a minstrel or a storyteller and a pet cat for stroking survive
and live on with the old woman. Creatures are born and die, but the
world goes on, and love between humans and animal life is a grace.
Colum subtly implies the unity and interdependence of life and he
inculcates a reverence for all living things.

The Frenzied Prince, Being Heroic Stories of Ancient Ireland (1943) is
the first children's book of Irish material. It is a collection of tales,
somewhat in the tradition of *The Arabian Nights,* told by the retainers
of King Donald to the seemingly mad Prince Suivne to remind him
of his nobility and help him to recover. Many of the stories are traditional Irish fare from the medieval epics such as "Cuchullain and
the Battle-Goddess," "Cuchullain and the Warrior Women." "The
Death of Cuchallain," and "How the Harp Came to Tara." The book
is not only reverential toward the legends of ancient Ireland, it is also
filled with very fine descriptions as when King Etercel's steward first
sees the beautiful maiden Esa: "What he saw held him fastened to
the limb of the tree. For within [the hut] was a girl more lovely than
any king's daughter: like whin blossom was her hair, like rowan ber-
ries her lips, like gentian flowers her eyes. And making her still more
lovely was the look she had, a look as if some dear companion was
beside her. But no one else was there, and the girl sang to herself as
she wove at the loom."[12]

The Frenzied Prince is an expensively produced book. The illustra-
tions, again by Willy Pogány, are magnificent. All in all, this late
book for children, Colum being in his sixties when he wrote it, is
one of the most visually and literarily satisfying of his many works
for young readers.

Except for *The Stone of Victory* (1966), a collection of previously published stories culled from seven books, Colum's last contribution to the fields of folklore, mythology, and children's literature is the mammoth collection of Irish legend, *A Treasury of Irish Folklore* (1954). It is a work that has become a standard reference in the field and it represents Colum's most serious effort to record and codify the folklore of his native country.

Technically, he edited rather than "wrote" *A Treasury of Irish Folklore*. Yet his incorporation of legend and myth in this book is only a little different from his treatment of this material in more "original" works such as *The King of Ireland's Son* or *The Frenzied Prince*. When in *A Treasury of Irish Folklore* Colum treats Irish myth, legend, the oral tradition, and distant history, he is once more the Circuit Poet telling his versions of ancient stories. When he is quoting from recent and contemporary historical sources, he is the judicious editor. Regardless, *A Treasury of Irish Folklore,* almost thirty years old at this writing, seems destined to remain the key reference work for those who wish to touch the soul of the Irish tradition.

A Treasury of Irish Folklore is divided into nine parts: "The Irish Edge" in which Colum tries to locate the essence of Irish imagination and humor through selected prose vignettes; "Heroes of Old" presents versions of the ancient Irish epics; "Great Chiefs and Uncrowned Kings" studies the victories and disasters of Irish history and ends in war cries in Gaelic; "Ireland without Leaders" treats with such catastrophes as the Insurrection of 1798. "New Leaders at Home and Abroad" is a delightful, sometimes serious, sometimes humorous treatment of such figures as Daniel O'Connell, Charles Stewart Parnell, Captain Boycott, Judge Lynch, John L. Sullivan, Michael Collins, and John McCormick; "Ways and Traditions" tells of the harp and the shamrock and the wearing of the green, also banshees, leprechauns, shillelaghs, and, of course, the potato; "Fireside Tales" are supernatural stories from various parts of Ireland; "The Fare of the Land" describes countryside and castle; "Ballads and Sons" presents Colum's selection of somewhat lesser known Irish songs along with the music and including, rightly, his own "She Moved through the Fair."

A Treasury of Irish Folklore is just that—a treasury: rich, varied, lavish, and overflowing. One would think that every Irish-American household would have a copy to remind all of the beauty, the joy, and the sorrow of the great Irish heritage.

In *Storytelling, New and Old* (1961) Colum restated his principles of children's literature first mentioned in *The Fountain of Youth* (1927):

> . . . The storyteller must have respect for the child's mind and the child's conception of the world, knowing it for a complete mind and a complete conception. If a storyteller have that respect he need not be childish in his language in telling stories to children. If the action be clear and the sentences clear one can use a mature language. Strange words, out-of-the-way words do not bewilder children if there be order in the action and in the sentences. They like to hear such words. Children love language for its own sake; they treasure words as they treasure keepsakes.[13]

Colum never lost his respect for children. As he loved and treasured words, so he remained steadfast in his belief that all children did so too.

Colum strongly believed that the main function of children's literature was to stimulate and expand the imaginative process in young readers:

> It is more important to let a child's imagination develop than it is to labor to inculcate in him or her some correct ethical point of view. If a child have in his or her mind the images that imaginative literature can communicate—the heroic, sweet, or loving types that are in the world's great stories—it is much more likely that he or she will grow up into a fine human being than if some austere mentor spoke to them out of every page of their reading. (*Sto*, 14–15)

The author hoped for a society that recognized the value of imagination:

> Some time, perhaps soon, it will come to be recognized that it is as important to cultivate the imagination as it is to cultivate the will or the intelligence. . . . For imagination is one of the great faculties; it is the one faculty common to all exceptional people—to soldiers, statesmen, saints; to artists, scientists, philosophers, and great business men. (*Sto*, 22–23)

Colum was convinced that literature was instructive; that the kindly teacher-writer-storyteller had a significant opportunity to develop character in the young. Furthermore, an imparting of a love for adventure could help create courageous young people who found life exciting: "With the mood of kindliness there should be the mood of adventure. The hero should be one who is willing to take strange paths in the morning and lie down under the giant's roof when the darkness falls" (*Sto*, 15).

Padraic Colum pursued a career in writing for children not merely because he was good at the work and he could earn a living by it. He wrote for the young because he was devoted to literature and therefore was deeply concerned with the growth and development of the reading audience. Children were for him, as for all of us, the hope of letters, the hope of the arts, the hope of the world. To write for the young was for Colum a sacred trust. He never violated it.

Only one major critic, Lionel Trilling, ever gave significant attention to Colum's writing for youth. Trilling recognized that Colum was making an educational contribution to Western culture. He appreciated Colum's high seriousness.[14] Lastly, Trilling probably hit on the secret of Padraic Colum's success as a children's writer:

Considering the preoccupations of the literary movement of his youth, nothing could be more appropriate than that he should tell the world's legends to our children. But he surely would not have told them so well, with so true a knowledge of how children should be spoken to, if he were content to speak only to children—if he did not, as poet, playwright, critic, and teacher, speak also, and as his first concern, to an adult audience. The best books for children are written by those who have something else to do, and do it well.[15]

Chapter Eight
Achievement and Summation

Padraic Colum was an Irish writer who wrote in English. His work was inextricably involved with the cultural and political revolution that led ultimately to the establishment of the Republic of Ireland. "In its subject matter Colum's [writing] takes account of the long, if undesirable presence of the Englishman on Irish soil."[1] He began as a playwright talking to his fellow Irish of the trials and tribulations, the hopes and aspirations, the pride and humility, the meanness and nobility of the Irish peasant. In his middle life he was a respected poet and a successful children's writer explaining Irish culture to the Anglo-Saxon world. In the end, long in years, he became, and he is remembered as an interpreter of an earlier, rural Ireland to succeeding generations of Irish men and women, girls and boys.

Growth and Development

Artistic success, popular recognition, and favorable critical attention came early to Colum, perhaps too early. By the time he was thirty years old he had contributed three major plays to the new Irish Theater: *The Land, The Fiddler's House,* and *Thomas Muskerry. Broken Soil,* the first version of *The Fiddler's House* was produced in 1903 when Colum was only twenty-one, and it was the initial success of the National Theatre Movement.

In 1907 his first book of poems, *Wild Earth,* seemed to indicate that a new star had risen in the brilliant firmament of the Irish Renaissance. In truth it turned out that he was more of a fiery comet that burned fiercely for a short while, seemed to grow cold, but in fact glowed on for sixty more creative years. As a young writer it was said that he had struck "a new note in Anglo-Irish poetry" and that he was "to be looked on as one of the most outstanding of those who were writing the verse of the future."[2]

The masculinity, the vividness, the rough impressionism of such poems as "The Plougher" and "A Drover" reminded readers of the robust Romanticism of Robert Burns. Colum the poet rebuffed the misty, soft, fading symbolism of the Celtic Twilight. His early poetry had some of the impact of John Masefield's *The Everlasting Mercy* (1911), the long narrative poem whose strong language and realistic subject matter shocked a reading public weaned on Victorian and Edwardian literary gentility. The reaction to and public debate over *The Everlasting Mercy* opened up a readership across the Irish Sea and the Atlantic Ocean to a writer like Colum whose peasant- and land-focused verse appealed to sensibilities cloyed with the sensuous and sometimes self-indulgent poetry of Algernon Swinburne, William Morris, and Dante Gabriel Rossetti. As Georgian tastes changed, the earthy lyrics of A.E. Housman grew more popular. Colum, perhaps a lesser poet than Housman, nevertheless was to Irish letters what Housman was to English letters: the vigorous poet writing about rural subjects, but in a simple, classical style.

In the theater Colum's disagreement with William Butler Yeats concerning the thrust and direction of the Abbey Theatre, along with his need to earn a living for his wife and himself, caused a breakup with the natural outlet for his drama. Eventually, after emigration to America, the roots connecting Colum to the Irish soil slowly withered. Although he tried over and over throughout his lifetime he was never again a successful professional playwright. The New York stage eluded his grasp to his great frustration.

Colum's poetry developed beyond *Wild Earth* in fits and starts; nevertheless, *Dramatic Legends, Old Pastures, Poems, Irish Elegies,* and *The Poet's Circuits* indicate a poetic maturation that eventually led to the remarkable late work, *Images of Departure.*

Colum became a creditable novelist in exile, even though he only wrote two. *Castle Conquer* and, especially, *The Flying Swans* continue to be widely read, the latter having achieved some recognition as one of the best studies of nineteenth-century rural Ireland. His work in children's literature and folklore shows that he took these areas most seriously and that he realized early that writing for the younger generation was an opportunity to give Irish children a proud knowledge of their culture and history, and the children of Europe and America insight into the myths and legends that helped form that culture called Western.

Padraic Colum lived by the pen. He was a professional writer, always willing, indeed eager, to accept new challenges and fresh assignments as the Hawaiian adventure best indicates. An aspect of his growth and development was his willingness, perhaps also his need, to take risks as with the biographical history, *Ourselves Alone,* and thus to venture into a difficult genre, primary history, with which he had had very little, if any, experience. He published about seventy-five books of poetry, drama, biography, fiction, children's literature, and folklore, as well as almost innumerable contributions to periodicals in criticism and history. He wrote successfully for more than seventy years. His poetry grew sharper and more personal with time. His prose became more poetic. He succeeded in unifying his thoughts and his feelings with his language. He was, in a word, a writer.

Achievement

Padraic Colum was a Catholic writer and thus different from the many Protestant Irish writers who did much to create the literary revival of modern Ireland. The discipline of his verse, his love of classicism, his concentration, his surety, and his unquestioning, unequivocating acceptance of the presence of God and the sanctity of the Church are all products of his background and a tribute to his faith. If Colum's God is imprecisely drawn and his belief implied but not stated, it is because he no more questioned the Deity or his institution on earth than he would ask about the air he breathed. In his delicate depictions of the landscape he loved, Colum included a priori his belief that God's hand had made the model for his images.

Colum was thus a poet of the senses, not an intellectual writer. He strove to reconstitute by his writing the sight and sound experiences of his youth. Psychological problems and metaphysical debates caused him little anxiety. It was enough to call life as he saw it and felt it. There was no Tennysonian crisis in Padraic Colum's life. He never doubted the existence of God, the reality of an afterlife, the coming independence of Ireland, and the greatness of Gaelic culture.

Colum loved, admired, and respected the peasant. In their long-suffering relationship with alien landlords, in their age-old struggle with the soil, in their deep-rooted love for the land, in their pride and their dignity, in their generosity and hospitability, in their courtesy and gentleness, and in their courage and stoicism, Colum saw the true nobility of humankind. "Colum's view of life is in essence that of the peasant as a noble savage endowed with the secrets of life and death. This valuable but somehow simple viewpoint is projected in poetry where not alone sowers and reapers but honey-sellers, drovers, blacksmiths, ballad-singers, bird-catchers, and tin whistle-players move in delightful but somehow silent mime."[3]

The poetry and fiction of Padraic Colum are a cultural bridge. They bring together the images and values of a people grown remote with time and the modern world of Ireland. Colum's adaptation of Gaelic speech rhythms and patterns into English verse and prose helps to unite the older Irish culture with the mainstream of English letters. Thus his work, including much of his children's literature, also serves as cultural history. In his rendering of the myths and folklore of Ireland specifically, and the myths and folklore of Europe generally, Colum was able to present and pass on in popular reading form the elemental building blocks of the literature and psychology shared by most of what is called the Western World.

Colum conceptionalized the modern Irish poet as a peasant bard, a preserver of the oral tradition, a storyteller with dramatic skill, a codifier of mores, and a conveyer of cultural values. In this concept he again identified conservatively with the past. The living poet, not the poem, is the personal link with ancient times. Today Colum's lyric poems are read and memorized by thousands of Irish schoolchildren yearly. Most often they do not learn or do not remember the author's name. They only know the poem is poetry from "older times," beautiful poems that tell them of and teach them about the past. Thus Padraic Colum has become both a national poet and an anonymous bard. It is exactly as he would have wished.

In his tribute to Padraic Colum Glenway Westcott said: "There are poetical writers who need to be taken as a unit, verse and prose, realistic novel and folklore, essay and drama, and by the same token, the personal fate and the remembrance. Padraic is typical of them; the whole is greater than the parts. There is no mystery in his work; the mystery was in him . . . and the names are love, humility, and almost priestly advocacy of literature every day of his life."[4]

Padraic Colum was a man who loved and admired women and in his work he treated them with affection, dignity, gentleness, and understanding. His mother was the primary influence on the writer when a boy, especially while his father was in America. She died young, and therefore Colum always remembered her as youthful, beautiful, and full of loving-kindness. The only other woman in his life was his wife Molly, the supporting, loving companion of a lifetime, whose great beauty in youth Colum never forgot and who thus remained the unchanging model of lovely woman in his work. As his belief in God was simple and direct, so was his faith in the goodness of women and their great service as a civilizing force in world affairs.

Influences

Unlike James Joyce in such work as *Dubliners* and *A Portrait of the Artist as a Young Man* Colum thought of his work as an opportunity to inculcate through example and implication a reverence for Irish culture, particularly that which stemmed from the Irish Catholic people of the countryside. Although he sometimes seemed to emphasize social conformity and sometimes was guilty of the advocacy of seemingly childlike virtues, nevertheless, more than most other Irish writers of his generation he understood the deepest feeling of the ordinary Irish people and like Synge and O'Casey he was able to give a realistic voice to that feeling, leaving "higher literature" to Yeats and others. "One tends, unwisely, to be deceived by the relative symplicity of Colum's verse."[5]

Without Colum's pioneering it is difficult to see how the realistic plays of Brendan Behan or the stories of Liam O'Flaherty and Frank O'Connor could have found the audience they did. Colum helped to connect Irish literature with the Irish people. A man of the masses, he always wrote for the masses. He helped to make realistic writing about the peasant respectable. No Irish writer made greater use of folk detail in so many genres and for so long a time. Thus a major influence of Colum now and for the foreseeable future is as a reference source for novelists, dramatists, artists, and actors seeking insights into the Irish past and information about customs, tradition, mores, attitudes, crafts, skills, clothing, food, family life, and, generally, all aspects of life in rural nineteenth-century and early twentieth-century Ireland.

In his novels, *Castle Conquer* and *The Flying Swans,* Colum did not merely espouse the cause of the Irish peasant against the overbearing and exploitative English landlords and rulers, he struck out for personal liberty and civil rights for all human beings. He demonstrably argued that all people are entitled to live in freedom and peace in their own country and be ruled by rulers of their own choice selected from their own number. In this regard Colum was a revolutionary writer speaking to all people striving for self-determination and dignity. As his peasants are his "nobles" so all peasants and workers in all societies are by implication the nobility of their own lands.

Finally, it must be noted that for a while Padraic Colum lived with giants: Yeats, Synge, Joyce; and later perhaps it made him seem taller. Nevertheless, Colum was a unique craftsman, working in almost every literary genre, producing quality work throughout a seventy-year writing career. He was a member of no school of poetry. He ran with no group or party. He was not a literary politician. If in his lifetime his literary reputation declined, he will not be forgotten as long as the people of Ireland and the worldwide descendants of the Irish want to remember the days of their ancestors. The poetry and prose of this most versatile of writers are destined to merge with Irish history.

Notes and References

Chapter One

1. Zack Bowen, *Padraic Colum* (Carbondale, Ill., 1970), 1–2.
2. Mary Colum, *Life and the Dream* (Garden City, N.Y., 1947), 64–65.
3. Bowen, *Colum*, 3.
4. Ibid., 2–3.
5. Ibid., 3.
6. Ibid., 4.
7. Colum, *Life and the Dream*, 94–95.
8. *The Road Round Ireland* (New York, 1926), 313.
9. See letter of 25 July 1911 to Mary Maguire following.
10. Taped interview with Zack Bowen, Easter 1966.
11. Bowen, *Colum*, 67.
12. As quoted in Lennox Robinson, *Ireland's Abbey Theatre: A History, 1899–1951* (Port Washington, N.Y. 1968), 38.
13. Lady Isabella Augusta Gregory, *Our Irish Theatre* (London, 1913), 20.
14. Peter Kavanagh, *The Story of the Abbey Theatre* (New York, 1950), 31–32.
15. Ibid., 34.
16. Mary and Padraic Colum, *Our Friend James Joyce* (Garden City, N.Y., 1958), 39.
17. Hugh Hunt, *The Abbey: Ireland's National Theatre, 1904–1979* (New York, 1979), 248. Also Robinson, *Abbey Theatre*, 31, 33.
18. Robert Hogan and Michael J. O'Neill, eds., *Joseph Holloway's Abbey Theatre: A Selection from His Unpublished Journal* (Carbondale, Ill., 1967), 60.
19. Robinson, *Abbey Theatre*, 43–44.
20. Kavanagh, *Story of the Abbey*, 58.
21. Hunt, *The Abbey*, 55.
22. Hogan and O'Neill, *Abbey Theatre*, 78.
23. Colum, *Life and the Dream*, 175.
24. Letter in Padraic Colum Collection, S.U.N.Y. Binghamton.
25. Bowen, *Colum*, 10.
26. Hogan and O'Neill, *Abbey Theatre*, 93.
27. Ibid., 155.
28. Ibid., 158.
29. Colum, *Life and the Dream*, 176.

30. Ibid., 220.

31. Bowen, *Colum,* 14.

32. Ibid., 15.

33. Charles Norman, *Ezra Pound* (New York: Funk & Wagnalls, 1969), 273.

34. *At the Gateways of the Day* (New Haven, 1924), xvi–xvii.

35. Bowen, *Colum,* 17.

36. Hogan and O'Neill, *Abbey Theatre,* 236.

37. Colum, *James Joyce,* 96.

38. Colum, *Life and the Dream,* 334.

39. Bowen, *Colum,* 18.

40. Colum, *James Joyce,* 201.

41. Ibid., 203, 209, 213.

42. Ibid., 235.

43. Ibid., 238–39.

44. Letter in Padraic Colum Collection, S.U.N.Y. Binghamton.

45. Bowen, *Colum,* p. 21.

46. Taped interview with Zack Bowen, Easter 1966.

47. Richard J. Loftus, *Nationalism in Modern Anglo-Irish Literature* (Madison, Wis., 1964), 317; hereafter cited as Loftus, *Nationalism.*

48. Allan Denson, "Padraic Colum: 1881–1972," *Capuchin Annual* (Dublin), 44 (1973), 52.

49. *The Road Round Ireland,* vi.

Chapter Two

1. As quoted by John L. Sweeney in *Collected Poems* by Padraic Colum (New York, 1953), v.

2. As quoted in Lady Gregory , *Our Irish Theatre,* 101.

3. *The Irish Independent* (8 December 1906), 4, as quoted in Robert Hogan and James Kilroy, *The Abbey Theatre: The Years of Synge, 1905–1909* (Dublin, 1978), 121.

4. Cornelius Weygandt, *Irish Plays and Playwrights* (New York, 1913; reprint, Westport, Conn., 1979), 207–8.

5. "The Talk of the Town," *New Yorker,* 9 June 1962, 25.

6. Robert Hogan and James Kilroy, *Laying the Foundations, 1902–1904* (Dublin, 1976), 47.

7. Robert Hogan and James Kilroy, eds., *Lost Plays of the Irish Renaissance* (Dixon, Calif., 1970), 65–71.

8. W. G. Fay and Catherine Carswell, *The Fays of the Abbey Theatre* (New York, 1935), 144–47.

9. Ernest Boyd, *The Contemporary Drama of Ireland* (Dublin, 1915), 112.

10. *Three Plays* (Dublin, 1917), p. 47; hereafter cited in text as *TP* followed by page number.

11. Richard Fallis, *The Irish Renaissance* (Syracuse, N.Y., 1977), 102.

12. Hunt, *The Abbey*, 53.

13. Letter of Padraic Colum (P. J. Columb) to W. B. Yeats. Ms. 10, 952, National Library of Ireland, as quoted in Hogan and Kilroy, *Laying the Foundations, 1902–1904*, 43.

14. Andrew E. Malone, *The Irish Drama* (London, 1929; reprint, New York, 1965), 167.

15. Una Ellis-Fermor, *The Irish Dramatic Movement* (London, 2d ed., 1954), 190.

16. As quoted in Bowen, *Colum*, 70. See also "The Irish National Theatre, New Play: *The Land*," *Freeman's Journal*, 10 June 1905, 8, as quoted in Hogan and Kilroy, *Abbey Theatre, 1905–1909*, 30–32.

17. Hogan and Kilroy, *Abbey Theatre, 1905–1909*, 251.

18. As quoted in Robinson, *Abbey Theatre*, 86. See "Miracle of the Corn," *Studies* (Dublin, 1907), 9–27.

19. Ibid.

20. Hunt, *The Abbey*, 91.

21. For the reviews of and responses to *Thomas Muskerry* see Robert Hogan, Richard Burnham, and Daniel P. Poteet, *The Abbey Theatre: The Rise of the Realists, 1910–1915* (Dublin, 1979), 26–33.

22. "Muskerryism–A Reply to 'X,' " *Sinn Fein* (23 July 1910), 3: as quoted in ibid., 30.

23. Ellis-Fermor, *Irish Dramatic Movement*, 191.

24. Ernest Boyd, *Ireland's Literary Renaissance* (New York, 1916, rev. 1922; reprint, New York, 1963), 341.

25. *Sinn Fein*, 28 July 1910, 1.

26. Malone, *Irish Drama*, 169.

27. "The Irish Literary Movement," *Forum* 53 (Jan. 1915): 145.

28. Ellis-Fermor, *Irish Dramatic Movement*, 7.

29. L. A. G. Strong, *Personal Remarks* (New York, 1953), 82.

30. As quoted by Charles Burgess, "A Playwright and His Work," *Journal of Irish Literature* 2, i (Jan. 1973): 43.

31. Bowen, *Colum*, p. 80.

32. The drafts of *Theodora*, Berg Collection, New York Public Library.

33. See "The Betrayal," J. W. Marriott, *One Act Plays of Today* (London: Harrop, 1928), 79–100.

34. As quoted in Zack Bowen, "Ninety Years in Retrospect: Excerpts from Interviews with Padraic Colum," *Journal of Irish Literature* 2, i (January, 1973): 30.

35. *Balloon* (New York, 1929), 13–14; hereafter cited in the text as *B* followed by page number.

36. As quoted in Bowen, "Ninety Years in Retrospect," p. 31.

37. *Moytura: A Play for Dancers* (Dublin, 1963). The other Noh plays of Colum are in manuscript with the Colum collection, S.U.N.Y. Binghamton.

38. Denson, "Padraic Colum, 1881–1972," 46.

39. "The Irish Peasant," *Evening Telegraph* (20 May 1911), 4; as quoted in Hogan, Burnham, and Poteet, *The Abbey Theatre*, 143.

Chapter Three

1. Fallis, *Irish Renaissance* 118.
2. Ibid., 120.
3. "Letter to a Young Poet," *Forum* 96 (Nov. 1936): X.
4. *Anthology of Irish Verse* (New York: Boni and Liveright, 1922, rev. 1948), 5–9.
5. As quoted in Loftus, *Nationalism*, 178.
6. Ibid., 179.
7. AE (George Russell) *New Songs* (Dublin: O'Donoghue, 1904), 5.
8. Loftus, *Nationalism*, 181.
9. Fallis, *Irish Renaissance*, 121.
10. Calvert Alexander, *The Catholic Literary Revival* (1933; reprint, Port Washington, N.Y., 1968), 270.
11. Fallis, *Irish Renaissance*, 119.
12. Boyd, *Ireland's Literary Renaissance*, 265.

Chapter Four

1. Strong, *Personal Remarks*, 79.
2. *Dramatic Legends and Other Poems* (New York, 1922), 99.
3. Bowen, *Colum*, 53.
4. *Old Pastures* (New York, 1930), vii.
5. Ibid.
6. Bowen, *Colum*, 46.
7. *The Story of Lowry Maen* (New York, 1937), viii.
8. Loftus, *Nationalism*, 170.
9. AE (George Russell), *Voices of the Stones* (London: Macmillan, 1925), vii.

Chapter Five

1. *The Poet's Circuits* (London, 1960), v; hereafter cited in the text as PC followed by page number.
2. Bowen, *Colum*, 41.
3. Bowen, *Colum*, 39.
4. Loftus, *Nationalism*, 190.

Chapter Six

1. *Castle Conquer* (New York, 1923), 38; hereafter cited in the text as *CC* followed by page number.
2. Bowen, *Colum,* 97.
3. *The Flying Swans* (Dublin: Allen Figgis, 1969), p. 454; hereafter cited in the text as *FS* followed by page number.
4. *Studies* (Dublin, 1907), 33–34; hereafter cited in the text as *St* followed by page number.
5. Bowen, *Colum,* 22.
6. Colum, *Our Friend James Joyce,* 6; hereafter cited in the text as *JJ* followed by page number.
7. *Ourselves Alone: The Story of Arthur Griffith and the Origin of the Irish Free State* (New York, 1959), v–vi; hereafter cited in the text as *OA* followed by page number.
8. *My Irish Year* (New York: James Pott, 1912), vii–viii; hereafter cited in the text as *IY* followed by page number.
9. Bowen, *Colum,* 117–18.
10. *The Road Round Ireland* (New York, 1926), 263; hereafter cited in the text as *RRI* followed by page number.
11. *Cross Roads in Ireland* (New York, 1930), 323; hereafter cited in the text as *CRI* followed by page number.
12. *A Half-Day's Ride; or Estates in Corsica* (New York, 1932), 7; hereafter cited in the text as *HDR* followed by page number.

Chapter Seven

1. Bowen, *Colum,* 125.
2. *The Adventures of Odysseus and the Tale of Troy* (New York, 1918), 252–54.
3. *The Boy Apprenticed to an Enchanter* (New York, 1920), 121–22.
4. *The Children of Odin* (New York, 1920), p. 264; hereafter cited in the text as *CO* followed by page number.
5. *The Six Who Were Left in a Shoe* (New York, 1968), 5.
6. *At the Gateways of the Day* (New Haven, 1924), xv; hereafter cited in the text as *AGD* followed by page number.
7. *The Bright Islands* (New Haven, 1925), 27.
8. Bowen, *Colum,* 126.
9. *Orpheus. Myths of the World* (New York, 1930), xxviii. The quotation is from Apollonius Rhodius: *The Argonautica,* Loeb Library, translated by R. C. Seaton.
10. *The White Sparrow* (New York, 1972), 13.
11. *Where the Wind Never Blew and the Cocks Never Crew* (New York, 1940), 94.

12. *The Frenzied Prince, Being Heroic Stories of Ancient Ireland* (Philadelphia, 1943), 31.

13. *Storytelling, New and Old* (New York, 1961), 13–14; hereafter cited in the text as *Sto,* followed by page number.

14. Lionel Trilling, "Mr. Colum's Greeks," *Griffin* (Christmas 1956), 11–12.

15. Ibid., 14–15.

Chapter Eight

1. Loftus, *Nationalism,* 178.

2. Alexander, *Catholic Literary Revival,* 268–69.

3. Bryan MacMahon, "Place and People in Poetry," *Irish Poets in English,* ed. Seán Lucy (Dublin: Mercier, 1973), 66.

4. Glenway Wescott, "Padraic Colum: 1881–1972," *Proceedings of the American Academy of Arts and Letters,* Second Series, no. 23 (1973): 92–93.

5. Robert Farren, "The Gaelic Voice in Anglo-Irish Poetry," *Irish Poets in English,* 136.

Selected Bibliography

PRIMARY SOURCES

1. Poetry

The Collected Poems of Padraic Colum. New York: Devin-Adair, 1953.

Creatures. New York: Macmillan, 1927.

Dramatic Legends and other Poems. New York and London: Macmillan, 1922.

Flower Pieces. Dublin: Orwell Press, 1938.

Images of Departure. Dublin: Dolmen Press, 1969.

Irish Elegies. Dublin: Dolmen Press, 1958, 1961, 1966 [second and third edition with changes].

Old Pastures. New York: Macmillan, 1930.

Poems. New York and London: Macmillan, 1932.

The Poet's Circuits. Collected Poems of Ireland. London: Oxford University Press, 1960.

The Story of Lowry Maen. New York and London: Macmillan, 1937.

Ten Poems. Dublin: Dolmen Press, 1957.

The Vegetable Kingdom. Bloomington, Indiana: Indiana University Press, 1954.

Wild Earth. A Book of Verse. Dublin: Maunsel, 1907.

Wild Earth, and Other Poems. New York: Holt, 1916.

2. Drama

Balloon. A Comedy in Four Acts. New York: Macmillan, 1929.

The Desert. Dublin: Devereux, 1912.

The Fiddler's House. Dublin: Maunsel, 1907.

The Land. Dublin: Abbey Theatre, 1905.

Mogu the Wanderer, or The Desert. Boston: Little, Brown, 1917.

Moytura: A Play for Dancers. Dublin: Dolmen, 1963.

Thomas Muskerry. Dublin: Maunsel, 1910.

Three Plays. The Fiddler's House, The Land, Thomas Muskerry. Dublin: Maunsel, 1917.

3. Fiction

Castle Conquer. New York and London: Macmillan, 1923.

The Flying Swans. New York: Crown, 1957.

Studies. Dublin: Maunsel, 1907.

Three Men. London: Elkin Mathews and Marrot, 1930.

4. Nonfiction

Cross Roads in Ireland. New York and London: Macmillan, 1930.
A Half-Day's Ride: or, Estates in Corsica. New York and London: Macmillan, 1932.
My Irish Year. London: Mills & Boon, 1912.
Our Friend James Joyce (by Padraic and Mary Colum). Garden City, N.Y.: Doubleday, 1958.
Ourselves Alone: The Story of Arthur Griffith and the Origin of the Irish Free State. New York: Crown, 1959.
The Road Round Ireland. New York: Macmillan, 1926.
Story Telling, New and Old. New York: Macmillan, 1961.

5. Children's Books and Folklore

The Adventures of Odysseus. New York: Macmillan, 1918.
At the Gateways of the Day. New Haven: Yale University Press, 1924.
The Big Tree of Bunlahy. Stories of My Own Countryside. New York: Macmillan, 1933.
The Boy Apprenticed to an Enchanter. New York: Macmillan, 1920.
A Boy in Eirinn. New York: E. P. Dutton, 1913.
The Boy Who Knew What the Birds Said. New York: Macmillan, 1918.
The Bright Islands. New Haven: Yale University Press, 1925.
The Children of Odin. New York: Macmillan, 1920.
The Children Who Followed the Piper. New York: Macmillan, 1922.
The Forge in the Forest. New York: Macmillan, 1925.
The Fountain of Youth. Stories to be Told. New York: Macmillan, 1927.
The Frenzied Prince, Being Heroic Stories of Ancient Ireland. Philadephia: McKay, 1943.
The Girl Who Sat By the Ashes. New York: Macmillan, 1919.
The Golden Fleece and the Heroes Who Lived Before Achilles. New York: Macmillan, 1921.
The Island of the Mighty. Being the Hero Stories of Celtic Britain Retold from the Mabinogion. New York: Macmillan, 1924.
The King of Ireland's Son. New York: Macmillan, 1916.
The Legend of Saint Columba. New York: Macmillan, 1935.
Legends of Hawaii. New Haven: Yale University Press, 1937.
Orpheus. Myths of the World. New York and London: Macmillan, 1930.
The Peep-Show Man. New York: Macmillan, 1924.
Six Who Were Left in a Shoe. London: Brentano, 1924; New York: McGraw-Hill, 1968.
The Stone of Victory and Other Tales of Padraic Colum. New York: McGraw-Hill, 1966.
The Voyagers. Being Legends and Romances of Atlantic Discovery. New York: Macmillan, 1925.

Where the Wind Never Blew and the Cocks Never Crew. New York: Macmillan, 1940.

The White Sparrow. New York: Macmillan, 1933.

SECONDARY SOURCES

1. Bibliography

Denison, Alan. *Padraic Colum: An Appreciation with a Checklist of His Publications.* Dublin Magazine 6, no. 1 (Spring 1967):50–67. Contains complete bibliography of all editions of Colum's books up through 1966.

2. Books

Alexander, Calvert. *The Catholic Literary Revival.* Milwaukee: Bruce, 1935. Reprint, Port Washington, N.Y.: Kennikat, 1968. Study of the religious roots of the Irish literary renaissance.

Bowen, Zack. *Padraic Colum. A Biographical-Critical Introduction.* Carbondale, Ill.: Southern Illinois University Press, 1970. Excellent overview of Colum's canon except for the very last works. Utilizes personal interviews with Colum.

Boyd, Ernest Augustus. *The Contemporary Drama of Ireland.* Dublin: Talbot, 1915. Early American study of the Abbey dramatists.

―――. *Ireland's Literary Renaissance.* New York: Knopf, 1916; rev. ed. 1922; reprint, New York: Barnes & Noble, 1968. Seminal study of the Irish literary renaissance by scholar personally acquainted with many of the authors.

Colum, Mary. *Life and the Dream.* Garden City, N.Y.: Doubleday, 1947. Wife's somewhat self-serving autobiography sheds light on Padraic Colum's lifestyle and methods of working.

Costello, Peter. *The Heart Grown Brutal.* Dublin: Gill & Macmillan, 1977. The interaction of the literary renaissance with the political revolution.

Ellis-Fermor, Una. *The Irish Dramatic Movement.* London: Methuen, 1939; rev. ed., 1954. Major critic summarizes the achievement of the movement and assesses the playwrights.

Fallis, Richard *The Irish Renaissance.* Syracuse, N.Y.: Syracuse University Press, 1977. Most valuable contemporary scholarly overview of Irish Renaissance.

Fay, W. G., and **Catherine Carswel.** *The Fays of the Abbey Theatre.* New York: Harcourt, Brace, 1935. Autobiographical record of the Abbey Theatre by a founder.

Gregory, Lady Isabella Augusta (Perse). *Our Irish Theatre*. London: Putnam, 1913. Personal account of involvement in the origins of the Irish Literary Theatre and the Abbey Theatre Company.

Hogan, Robert, Richard Burnham, and Daniel P. Poteet. *The Abbey Theatre: The Rise of the Realists, 1910–1915*. Dublin: Dolmen, 1979. Part of documentary series re-creating growth and development of modern Irish drama through journals, reviews, and letters.

Hogan, Robert and James Kilroy. *The Abbey Theatre: The Years of Synge, 1905–1909*. Dublin: Dolmen, 178. Part of above series.

———. *Laying the Foundations, 1902–1904*. Dublin: Dolmen, 1976. Part of above series.

———, eds. *Lost Plays of the Irish Renaissance*. Dixon, Calif.: Proscenium Press, 1970. Contains *The Saxon Shillin'*.

Hogan, Robert, and Michael J. O'Neill, eds. *Joseph Holloway's Abbey Theatre: A Selection from His Unpublished Journal*. Carbondale, Ill.: Southern Illinois University Press, 1967. Useful and delightful selection from Holloway's "Impresions of a Dublin Playgoer." Firsthand impressions of performances and playwrights.

Hunt, Hugh. *The Abbey, Ireland's National Theatre, 1904–1979*. New York: Columbia University Press, 1979. Fine, up-to-date history of Abbey Theatre.

Kavanagh, Peter. *The Story of the Abbey Theatre*. New York: Devin-Adair, 1950. A polemic study of history of Abbey emphasizing struggle against mendacity and censorship.

Loftus, Richard J. *Nationalism in Modern Anglo-Irish Poetry*. Madison. Wis.: University of Wisconsin Press, 1964. Study of the twentieth-century Irish poets who identified with Irish cultural traditions and political aspirations.

Malone, Andrew E. *The Irish Drama*. London: Constable, 1929; reprint, New York: Bloom, 1965. Celebrates twenty-fifth anniversary of the Abbey Theatre.

Robinson, Lennox. *Ireland's Abbey Theatre: A History, 1899–1951*. London: Sidgwick & Jackson, 1951; reprint, Port Washington, N. Y.: Kennikat, 1968. Documentary history by one of the Abbey's great directors and playwrights.

Strong, L. A. G. *Personal Remarks*. New York: Liveright, 1953. Generous words about Colum's poetry.

Weygandt, Cornelius. *Irish Plays and Playwrights*. New York: Houghton Mifflin, 1913; reprint, Westport, Conn.: Greenwood, 1979. Early study of Irish Renaissance playwrights.

3. Articles

Bowen, Zack. "Ninety Years in Retrospect: Excerpts from Interviews with Padraic Colum." *The Journal of Irish Literature* 2, no. 1 (January 1973):

14–34. Colum's memories of Irish Renaissance figures and of his own life and work.

Denson, Alan. "Padraic Colum: 1881–1972." *Capuchin Annual* (Dublin) 1973, pp. 45–54. Generous appreciation of Colum the man.

Trilling, Lionel. "Mr. Colum's Greeks." *The Griffin* (Christmas, 1956), pp. 4–15. Admires Colum's ability as writer for children.

Westcott, Glenway. "Padraic Colum: 1881–1972." *Proceedings of the American Academy of Arts and Letters,* 2d ser., no. 23 (1973): 87–93. Eulogy and appreciation by colleague.

Index

Abbey Theatre Company, 6, 7, 8, 15, 16, 29
Academy of American Poets, 21
Adventures of Odysseus, The, 131
AE (George Russell), 4, 6, 10, 22, 44, 84
Anderson, Sherwood, 13
At the Gateways of the Day, 16

Balloon, 17, 37–38
Beckett, Samuel, 39
Betrayal, The, 11, 36–37
Big Tree of Bunlahy, The, 138–39
Boer War, 5, 24
Boy Apprenticed to an Enchanter, The, 132
Boy in Eirinn, A, 130
Boy Who Knew What the Birds Said, The, 131
Bright Islands, The, 16
Broken Soil, 6, 24–26; name, meaning of, 24
Brooks, Van Wyck, 13

Carnegie School of Drama, 12
Casement, Roger, 14
Castle Conquer, 14, 16, 106–10, 148
Catholic World, 121
Catholicism, Irish, 1
Children of Odin, 133
Children Who Followed the Piper, The, 134
Collected Poems (1953), 21, 76–80; "Achill Girl's Song," 77, 78; "Charm, The," 78; "City Clocks, The," 79; "Old Song Re-sung, An," 77
Colum, Josephine, 12
Colum, Mary, 1
Colum, Padraic, as actor, 6; as chronicler of old, not new, Ireland, 14, 146–48; as first of the Irish realists, 26; as shaper of American opinion

about Ireland, 14–15; children's literature, involvement in, 13–14; civil war, response to, 11; dramatist, limitation as, 23; emigration to the U.S., 12–13; Hawaiian folklore assignment, 15–16; honors to, 21; influence of AE on poetry, 4, 22, 44, 48; local color, use of, 4, 23, 25–26, 74–75, 108, 109, 123, 146–47; patriotism, 44; Poetry Society of America Medal, 20; religious beliefs, 146–47; renaming, significance of, 4; response to London, 3–4; style of, 106–107; support of siblings, 3; technique of, 26–27, 46 (*see also* local color, use of; WORKS); Yeats, falling out with, 7, 145

WORKS:
Adventures of Odysseus, The, 131
At The Gateways of the Day, 16, 135–36
Balloon, 17, 37–38
Betrayal, The, 11, 36–37
Big Tree of Bunlahy, The, 138–39
Boy Apprenticed to an Enchanter, The, 132
Boy in Eirinn, A, 130
Boy Who Knew What the Birds Said, The, 131
Bright Islands, 16, 135–36
Broken Soil, 6, 24–26
Castle Conquer, 14, 16, 106–10, 148
Children of Odin, 133
Children Who Followed the Piper, The, 134
Collected Poems (1953), 21, 76–80
Creatures, 17, 64–67
Cross Roads in Ireland, 125
Desert, The, 34, 35–36
Dramatic Legends and Other Poems, 16, 59–64

"Drover, A," 46, 47, 144
Fiddler's House, The, 9, 24–27
Flower Pieces, The, 20, 75–76
Flying Swans, The, 20, 109–12, 145,
    148
Forge in the Forest, The, 17, 137
Frenzied Prince, The, 20, 140
Girl Who Sat by the Ashes, The,
    131–32
*Golden Fleece and the Heroes Who Lived
    before Achilles,* 133–34
Half-Day's Ride, A, 126–28
Images of Departure, 21, 100–105
Irish Elegies (1958, 1961, 1963), 21,
    85–88
Island of the Mighty, 134
King of Ireland's Son, The, 13, 130
Land, The, 7, 27–29
Legend of Saint Columba, The, 139
Legends of Hawaii, 16
Miracle of the Corn, The, 9, 28–29
My Irish Year, 121–24
Noh Plays, 38–43
Old Pastures, 67–71
Orpheus, 17, 138
Our Friend James Joyce, 20, 114–18
*Ourselves Alone: Arthur Griffith and the
    Origins of the Irish Free State,* 20,
    119–21
Peep-Show Man, The, 135
"Plougher, The," 46, 47, 144
Poems (1932), 17, 71–73
Poet's Circuits, The, 21, 88–100
"Portrait, A," 46
Road Round Ireland, The, 15, 17,
    121, 123–25
Saxon Shillin', The, 5, 23–24
Six Who Were Left in a Shoe, 135
Story of Lowry Maen, The, 73–75
Storytelling, New and Old, 142
Studies, 112–13
Ten Poems, 82–84
"Theodora," 36
Thomas Muskerry, 9, 29–33
Three Men, 114
Treasury of Irish Folklore, A, 141
Vegetable Kingdom, The, 80–82
Voyagers, The, 17, 137
White Sparrow, The, 139

Wild Earth, 9, 13, 48–52, 144
Wild Earth and Other Poems (1916),
    54–59

Columbia University, 19
Commonweal, 121
Cosgrave, William, 15
Creatures, 17, 64–67; "Asses," 65;
    "Crows," 65; "Jackdaw," 65; "Plov-
    ers," 65; "Swallow," 66
Cross Roads in Ireland, 125

Desert, The, 34, 35–36
Dial, 121
Dramatic Legends and Other Poems, 16,
    59–64; "Bird of Paradise, The," 62;
    "Lament," 60; " Men on Islands,"
    60; "Monkeys, The," 63; "Poor
    Girl's Meditation," 60–61; "Wild
    Ass, The," 61–62
"Drover, A," 46–47, 144
Dublin Magazine, 121

Fays (theatrical group), 6, 9
Ferguson, Samuel, 45
Fiddler's House, The, 9, 24–27; Irish
    peasant character, depiction of, 26;
    male sexual power, expression of, 25;
    name, meaning of, 24
Flower Pieces, 20, 75–76; "Acanthus
    leaves," 76; "Hollyhocks," 75;
    "Morning Glories," 75; "Poppies,"
    76
Flying Swans, The, 20, 109–12, 145,
    148; use of language, 111–12
Forge in the Forest, The, 17, 137
Forum, 19
Freeman's Journal, 11
Frenzied Prince, The, 20, 140
Frost, Robert, 12

Gaelic American, 12
Gaelic League, 4
Gaiety Theatre, 5
Girl Who Sat by the Ashes, The, 131–32
*Golden Fleece and the Heroes Who Lived
    before Achilles,* 133–34
Gonne, Maud, 5, 6

Grasshopper, The (collaboration with
  E.W. Freund), 15
Greene, Emmet, 20
Gregory, Lady Isabella Augusta, 5, 7,
  11, 22
Griffith, Arthur, 4, 14; *See also Ourselves
  Alone*

Half-Day's Ride, A, 126–28; "Marine
  Adventure, A," 126, 127; "Miss Europe," 126–27; Horniman, Elizabeth, 7, 9, 30
Houston, David, 10

Images in Departure, 21, 100–105;
  "After Speaking of One Who Died a
  Long Time Before," 102; "Day's
  End," 103; "Discovery," 104; "Ex-
  pecting No One," 101–102; "Forget
  Me Nots," 102; "Images of Depar-
  ture," 101; "In Saint Stephen's
  Green," 103; "Name and Legend,"
  103; "New Legend," 102
Ionesco, Eugene, 39
Ireland: attitude toward British in late
  1880s, 2; civil war, threat of, 11;
  modern drama, beginnings of, 5;
  partition of, 14; poverty in late
  1880s, 1–2
Ireland, Theatre of, 9
Irish Elegies (1958, 1961, 1963), 21,
  85–88; "Artificer, James Joyce,
  The," 86–87; "Magister, Monsignor
  Padraig De Brun, The," 87;
  "Painter, John Butler Yeats, The,"
  85–86; "Player, Dudley Digges,
  The," 87; "Poet, Seamus O'Sullivan,
  The," 87; "Rebel, Roger Casement,
  The," 85; "Stateman, Arthur Grif-
  fith, The," 86
Irish Free State, 14
Irish Independent, 4, 5
Irish Literary Theatre, 5
Irish National Clearing House, 4
Irish National Theatre Society, 6, 16,
  22, 23, 144
Irish Republican Brotherhood, 4
Irish Review, 10

Irish Times, 11
*Island of the Mighty, Being the Hero Sto-
  ries of Celtic Britain Retold,* 134

Joyce, James, 3–4, 6, 15, 16–17; *See
  also Our Friend James Joyce*

Kelly, Thomas Hughes, 9
King of Ireland's Son, The (collaboration
  with Pogany), 13, 130

Land, The, 7, 27–29; soil as character,
  28; tragedy of loss, expression of, 28
League, Gaelic, 4
Legend of Saint Columba, The, 139–40
Legends of Hawaii, 16
Lindsay, Vachel, 13
Literary Theatre, Irish, 5
Lowell, Amy, 13

MacDonagh, Thomas, 10
McDowell, Colony, 14
McGrath, Joseph, 20
Macmillan Publishers, 13–14
Maguire, Mary Gunning, 9, 10
Manchester Guardian, 11, 121
Mangan, James Clarence, 45
Martyn, Edward, 5
Masters, Edgar Lee, 13
Maugham, Somerset, 13
Mechanics Theatre, 7
Miracle of the Corn, The, 9, 28–29
Monroe, Harriet, 13
Moody, Harriet, 12
Moore, George's, 5, 10
Moore, Thomas, 45
Mulcahy, Richard, 15
My Irish Year, 121–24

Nation, 121
New Songs, 46
New Statesman, 11
Noh Plays, 38–43; as invocation of
  mood, 39; cycle of five: "Cloughoughter," 40, 41; "Glendalough,"
  40; "Kilmore," 40, 42; "Monasterboice," 40, 42; *Moytura,* 40

O'Casey, Sean, 7, 8, 16, 22
Old Pastures, 67–71; "At the Fore of the Year," 68–69; "Blades," 70; "Dublin Roads," 67; "Fuchsia Hedges in Connacht," 67–68; "Lilac Blossoms," 68; "Man Bereaved, A," 68, 69; "Odysseus," 70–71; "Scanderbeg," 68, 69; "Song of Starlings," 70
O'Neill, Eugene, 17
Orpheus, 17, 138
Our Friend James Joyce, 20, 114–18
Ourselves Alone: Arthur Griffith and the Origins of the Irish Free State, 20, 119–21

Pearse, Padraic, 4
Peep-Show Man, The, 135
Perkins, Maxwell, 17
"Plougher, The," 46–47, 144
Poems (1932), 18, 71–73; "Knitters, The," 71–72; "Laburnums," 72; "Saint, A," 72
Poetry, 13
Poetry Society of America, 12, 20
Poet's Circuits, The, 21, 88–100; structure of, 89; "Call for the Bride, The," 96–97; "Fore-piece," 89–90; "Hired Scythesman," 91–92; "May Day," 94; "Old Woman Selling Ducks," 96; "Raftery," 95; "Spadesman," 92; "Storyteller," 90–91
Pogany, Willy, 13
"Portrait, A," 46
Pound, Ezra, 15

Revival, Celtic, 8
Road Round Ireland, The, 15, 121, 123–25
Robinson, Edwin Arlington, 13
Robinson, Lennox, 29
Russell, George (AE), 4, 6, 10, 22, 44, 84

Sandburg, Carl, 13
Saturday Review of Literature, 121
Saxon Shillin', The, 5, 23–25; expression of historic Irish dilemma, 24;

inflammatory nature of, 24; name, meaning of, 5
Sinn Fein, 4
Six Who Were Left in a Shoe, 135
Story of Lowry Maen, The, 73–75
Storytelling, New and Old, 142
Studies, 112–13; "Eilis: A Woman's Story," 112–13; "Flute Player's Story, The," 113
Sunday Tribune (New York), 13
Synge, John Millington, 7, 8, 22
Ten Poems, 82–84; "Basket-Maker, The," 83; "Book of Kells, The," 82; "Egan O'Rahilly," 84; "Hearthstone and the Loom, The," 83; "On Not Hearing the Birds Sing in Ireland," 83; "Road, A Garden and a Summer Evening, A," 83
Theatre, Abbey, 6, 7, 8, 15, 16, 29; conflict over purpose of Irish drama, 8; size of, 7–8; themes of plays, 8
Theatre of Ireland, 9
"Theodora," 36
Thomas Muskerry, 9, 29–33; as battlefield for critics, 30; characterization, 32; setting, 31; portrayal of old age, 33
Three Men, 114
Treasury of Irish Folklore, A, 141

United Irishman, 4, 5, 24, 44, 114

Valera, Eamon de, 14
Vegetable Kingdom, The, 80–82; "Catalpa Tree," 80; "Flowering Quince," 81; "Stocks or Pinks or Gillyflowers," 81; "Sunflower," 80; "Tiger Lilies," 81; "To Saint Fiacre, Patron of Gardens," 81
Voyagers, The, 17, 137

Welles, Orson, 35
White Sparrow, The, 139
Wild Earth, 9, 13, 48–52, 144; "Across the Door," 50; "Ballad Maker, A," 52; "Connachtman," 51; "Dermott Donn MacMorna," 49; "Good Men of Eirinn, The," 50;

"No Child," 50–51; "Old Woman of the Roads, An," 49; "Seed," 51; "Suilier, The," 50; "Young Girl, The," 49
Wild Earth and Other Poems (1916), 54–59; "Baltimore Exile," 56; "Carricknabauna," 55; "For Morfydd," 58–59; "I Shall Not Die for Thee,"

57; "Old Men Complaining," 58; "Parrot and the Falcon, The," 58; "River Mates," 55; "She Moved Through the Fair," 55; "Three Spinning Songs," 55

Yeats, William B., 4–9, 22, 145